Staying Joyfully Married... My LITTLE BOOK OF

"What-Nots"

Tena L. Nance (Parker)

ISBN:
Paperback: 978-1-969367-09-0
Hardback: 978-1-969367-10-6
e-Book: 978-1-969367-11-3

Printed in the United States of America

Contents

Life is not always about the mistakes you have made. It is about how you learn from those mistakes that is the lesson. To God be the glory that I am still continuing to become...

Papa, I did the best I could. Thank you for inscribing in my heart to always look to the hills...
Psalm 121

Introduction

Affirmations...

God speaks. If you listen. I can admit that whenever I made the "time" to listen, I could hear God's small still voice. When I got rid of the noise, I could hear God's voice. When I removed myself from the 'busyness' of the world, I could hear God's voice. When I got somewhere and settled myself down, I could hear God's voice. It is funny how some of us, including me, only make ourselves "available" when we need something from God. When we need God to "shake some things up." Or when we need God to "move this" or "move that." To "add this" or "remove that." That's when we become prayer warriors or prayer walers because we have an urgent need from God and we need Him to come into our situation. And we would prefer if God would move rather quickly on our behalf. That is when we become ALL ears. Intentionally trying to listen to God at every moment in our day. Just waiting to hear something. Anything. All the while, thoughts are erratically consuming your day. Thoughts like, "What do I do? What don't I do? What do I say? What don't I say? How do I act? How don't I act?" I did not know this role. And not only did I not know this role, but it was also an unexpected and very uncomfortable role. When my husband and I separated in 2019, I became one of those 'ones' that became ALL ears. Just wanting, needing, and anticipating a 'mighty move' by the Hand of God. I so desperately needed to hear a Word from God. The family I had once known had dissipated. And honestly, I did not know this season.

3

Since I met my husband almost 20 years ago, I had never been physically separated from him for any extended period of time. We did EVERYTHING together. So yes, this season was really unfamiliar for me. Real uncomfortable for me. Real trying for me. Real opaque for me. What had our world come to? Living independently? What does that mean? Do we talk? Do we not talk? Do we see each other? Do we stay away from each other? What are the rules to this game? I have never played before. Who establishes the rules? What comes next? I can tell you what came next. We are so independent that we live in two different cities establishing 'new beginnings.' Such 'new beginnings' that are independent of one another. Over time, I thought our conversation would have gotten better with time. But it did not. Seemed like time was growing us further and further apart. So apart to the point that we had little or no communication with one another. And when we did communicate, it was so "matter-of-fact" and succinct. No small talk. No emotions. No feelings. Just line-by-line and precept-by-precept talking. This became my 'norm.' So, you can only imagine how challenging this situation became for me. And, since I am being candid, it seemed like I spent more days in the valley than on the mountain tops. Seemed like I had more dark days than light ones. Seemed like my weeping endured for longer than just a night. Seemed like grave clothes became my daily attire. Seemed like I could not pull myself 'up.' No matter what I tried. Listening to encouraging messages only helped for a little while. Listening to uplifting music only helped for a while. I would try this, and I would try that. Until I literally exhausted myself trying. Remember when I said that God speaks? Well, when I got tired of being sick and tired. When I felt like I could not go any further. I sat my worried self-down and listened. God spoke. And, what He spoke, changed my entire being. God told me that everything that "I" was doing, was only going to last for a little while. I was only going to get temporary results from my own efforts. God told me that "I" was the problem. "I" was trying to "fix" the broken. "I" was trying to "mend" the broken-hearted. "I" was trying to "rebuild" the broken bridges. "I", "I", "I". I was making this all about "I". That is why I was exhausting myself. I was trying to do a job outside of my capabilities. And God would let me tire myself until

I realized that "I" cannot do HIS job. Yikes! That is why my efforts were not working. That is why I was becoming physically, spiritually, emotionally, and mentally drained. I was trying to resolve things the same way I had been doing my entire life. I was subtly removing God out of the picture. Yet I was asking Him to move this mountain in my marriage. Instead of letting go and letting God, I was holding on and wishing on Tena. Wishing that I could make things better. Wishing that I could erase the mistakes. Wishing that I could bandage up the pain. Wishing that I could patch up the wounds. Wishing that I could come in and 'save all.' I was trying to be a savior. But THAT position has already been taken. Yet, me being me, I still wanted to try. God is the only One who can "fix" or "heal" the broken. God is the only One who can "mend" the broken-hearted. God is the only One who can "rebuild" broken bridges. Not me. I played my part in helping 'break' some things. And in my finite mind, I thought I could come in and make things all better. Not. This situation was different. This warfare was different. Which means something different was going to have to be done. This was bigger than a little pity pat prayer. I could not expect different results if I were not willing to do something different.

While in prayer one morning, God reminded me of the place "He" wants to be in my life. HE does not want to come behind me after I have exhausted all of my options. HE does not want to play second fiddle to anyone. And HE definitely does not want to be my last option after I had my hand in messing everything up. Trusting God meant having to take my hands off of it completely. And just trust. And, if I was even considering not trusting or doubting God, He began to show me some things. He showed me how the enemy tried to destroy me in this season alone. The enemy tried to kill my joy. My hope. My trust. My health. My expectations. My marriage. My faith in God. The enemy tried to convince me that God did not love me because if He did, then I would not be going through what I am going through right now. That deviant little snake was seeking to devour me (1 Peter 5:8). He was trying to KILL me. Do you not understand how humbling it is that God spared me? Do you not understand that God does answer prayers? As a little girl, I remember I would ask God to protect me from dangers seen and unseen. It got so routine for me that I continued that practice in my prayers as an adult. But there is a humility when you find out that your little 'routine' prayer actually had been protecting you. You know. That prayer you did not put that much thought into. That prayer you just were accustomed to saying because your grandmama made you say it. That prayer that you do not even realize you say because it is so common and general for you. But God. Do you not understand how humbling it is that God used ALL that the enemy tried to use to kill me with, to grow me? Do you not understand how humbling it is that during this COVID-19 season, thousands and thousands of people have lost their loved ones? YET, it is during this season that God has saved me? And has allowed me to still be here to testify of His grace and mercy. Do you not understand how humbling it is that during this COVID-19 season that while many are in financial struggle(s) that God has kept me in this season? God is Jehovah-Jireh ("The Lord will provide"). We are in a season of famine, but God has provided me with more than enough. Do you not understand how humbling it is that while people are by the thousands, God has allowed this season to be my "birthing" season? Yes. What the world calls this "dry" season. However, this has been my birthing season because even though my circumstances have changed, the seeds that God has put on the inside of me, have manifested. Birthing season because even though my environment is not favorable, my purpose has not changed. "For I know the plans I have for you," declares the Lord, "plans to prosper you and not to harm you, plans to give you hope and a future" (Jeremiah 29:11). God has accounted for my every misstep. God has accounted for my every mistake. God has accounted for my every wrong turn. God has accounted for this pandemic. Do you not understand how humbling it is that God has long suffered with me? Do you not understand how humbling it is that God could have gotten anyone else to fulfill His assignment? Yet, knowing ALL that He knows about me, He STILL chose me? Do you not understand how humbling it is that God has drawn something out of me that I HAD NO IDEA was even in me? Do you not understand how humbling it is that God trusts me with His seed? And, during a pandemic. Do you not understand how humbling it is that God has been LOYAL since before my Day 1 debut on this earth? I could go on and on and on. But you get it.

God has an untraditional way of doing things sometimes. Because as I just mentioned, it was in this season, that God drew something out of me that nobody could have convinced me that I even had on the inside of me. But I had to do my part first. Once I exposed my heart and became transparent in front of God, He was able to "go to work." "Go to work" at healing my heart. "Go to work" at healing my mind. "Go to work" at healing my spirit. "Go to work" at healing my body. And God, being untraditional, told me that He was going to use these same "exposures" to bring me exposure. Exposure to His Truth. Exposure to His Grace. Exposure to His Mercy. Exposure to His Healing. And He was going to do this by my obedience in owning and standing in my truth. This "exposure" was not easy. And this "exposure" was kind of ugly. But this "exposure" was the beginning of me living my life transparently before God. Transparent before myself. Transparent before my husband. Transparent in my life. Transparent before you.

In my book called, "Growing Up In Marriage...Perfectly Flawed," I talk a lot about this process of exposure. Exposure leading to transparency. And transparency leading to truth. And it was in this truth that God's healing ensued. Initially, I thought this book was going to be about my marriage. And it was. Just not as much as I thought. This book was more about me and how I chose to deal with the hand that I was dealt. This book was predominantly about dealing with the issues of "me." The issues of "me" that I was confronted with early on in childhood that helped to shape the 'perfectly loved' and 'perfectly flawed' woman that is before you today. This book was hard in itself to write because I was not writing about someone else or even a fictional character. "I" was the main character. This chick was real. This chick had issues. This chick was broken. This chick made some HUGE mistakes. This chick was embarrassed. This chick was ashamed. This chick was guilty. This chick was a whole lot of things. And when God informed me that I was going to have to spill the 'tea' publicly, I was like, "Really God?" And so softly. So subtly. God asked me one little question, "How bad do you want your healing? Do you want it bad enough to burst the bubble you have been living in? Do you want it bad enough to tear down the 'wall of facade' you have shown people? Do you want it bad enough to show the world the 'real' broken, unhealed, vulnerable you? The 'real' you that "I" say you are. And not the 'you' defined by your mistakes. Do you not believe that I can take all your mistakes and use them for your good? So again, I ask you, 'How bad do you want it'?" All this time, I thought I was just releasing by writing for my own therapy. Wrong. When God gave me my instructions, well, let us just say, it was hard for me to breathe. But no matter how I may have tried to change God's mind, I knew deep down I was going to have to fulfill this assignment. The one thing I have learned is that when God tells me to do something, I better get to it because being obedient is so much better than the unexpected or unwilling sacrifice I may end up enduring (1 Samuel 15:22).

So, here I was thinking that once this assignment was fulfilled, I was done. My assignment was complete. Not quite. Again, God is NOT traditional. God has SO MANY different facets that we are not able to even imagine or comprehend. God has SO MANY different people He can use to vocalize His Message of love, salvation, forgiveness, and grace in the earth realm. Just sit back, relax, and take it all in.

As I was in the mirror one morning declaring my daily affirmations over my day, one thing I declared was, "I am happily married." And almost immediately, something stirred in my spirit. Here is how it was explained to me. Being happy is a temporary state of being. Happiness is something that you can control. Happiness is not absolute. It is a variable which is oftentimes based on a condition, a circumstance, or even the environment. Happiness is something that you can regulate. Happiness can be something that can be predicated on the temperature of something else. So, instead of declaring, "I AM happily married," I was instructed to declare "I AM joyfully married." The Holy Spirit explained to me that joy is NOT a temporary state of being. Joy is NOT something we can control. Joy IS an absolute. When everything around you is changing God's, joy does not. Joy is: 1) A gift from God that we did not do anything to earn or deserve. And 2) Joy is a gift that God will not take back. God is not a man that He should lie; neither the son of man that He should repent (Numbers 23:19). When you declare an emotion like 'happiness' over

8

your marriage, then 'happiness' is what you will get. Do not get me wrong, there is nothing wrong with wanting happiness. For we all have this desire. However, would you rather have something absolute in your life over something that is variable? Something concrete and secure versus something shaky and conditional? Although life changes, God's joy does not change. Although you may lose something or someone, God's joy does not change. Although you may encounter some mountains or some unexpected struggles in your life, God's joy does not change. It is up to us whether or not we accept God's gift. For me, having joy will trump ascertaining happiness every time.

So, upon your declaration that you are 'joyfully' married, when things become out of alignment to God's Word, go back to The Source. Not your husband. Not yourself. Not your girlfriends. Not your family members. You need to go back to God. When God makes you a promise, He is more than well and able to fulfill it. God is intentional about how He chooses to bless you. And, when your marriage becomes 'un-joyful' and not in alignment of what God has promised, go back to God. Go back to God for wisdom. Go back to God for guidance. Go back to God for direction. Go back to God in submission. If you remember WHO gives you joy, then you will remember WHO holds the blueprint on how your marriage should look. Your spouse cannot give you joy. Having 'stuff' cannot give you joy. Having 'titles' cannot give you joy. Having a relationship with God is the only thing that can give you the joy you need to be able to sustain. Once you make God your "WHO," then that subservient attitude will spill over into every other relationship you have, including your marriage. Once you make God your "WHO", then you start chasing after Him like no other. And you begin to look like Him. You start displaying the character of God. And once you give God your heart (i.e., His Kingdom on the inside of you), all other things (i.e., your marriage) will be added unto you (Matthew 6:33). When you allow God to take the driver's seat of your marriage, and take capture of those temporary emotions (i.e., happiness), then you will be less easily deceived out of the permanent emotion of joy that God says belongs to you (Psalm 16:11).

Sounds like pretty good advice, right? Here lies my dilemma. Hello? Did I mention that I am separated? Like really separated? Was I getting punk'd? How was I going to tell someone how to stay 'joyfully' married when I was only married on paper? How was I going to tell someone how to keep happiness, joy, or any other emotion in their marriage, for that matter? God, are you sure you chose the right person? God, you know I felt like a hypocrite trying to tell someone else what to do in their marriage. God, you know I did not always follow my own instructions. God, if I knew how to stay 'joyfully' married, would not I BE 'joyfully' married? God, I could not possibly try to enlighten someone else in their marriage journey when mine had been macheted. I am not a leader in this area. God, I know You are Omniscient (All-Knowing) and all creating, but have you taken a look at my marriage lately? Hello? I am living in the evidence. I was so confused. Yet, with every ounce of my being, I was trying to be obedient. But was I afraid? Absolutely. Was I given all the instructions? Was I told how this thing would all turn out? Did I believe that I was supposed to "rise up" out of this set of ashes? I may not have always felt like it. But The Word said that I would (Isaiah 61:3). But if I am all in, then I am all in. I have to trust God. Then I have to trust God. POINT. BLANK. PERIOD.

So, with this assignment, much prayer and meditation was needed. Did I mention how I believe God has an untraditional sense of humor? Well, I think He does. Because, in the midst of all of my beautiful mixture of confusion, I encountered this young woman. A stranger. A newly engaged young woman just randomly at the store. I was not trying to engage in any conversation. And especially not about marriage. I was trying to get in. Get out. Get what I needed. And leave. I was particularly and intentionally trying to 'hide in the shadows' and go unnoticed. But God. All I can say is that God has a special way. A special and strategic way of doing things. Because in my mind, I was obviously NOT the best person to give advice or wisdom about anything; let alone marriage. But again. God with His humor. I thought me and this young woman were just having a random 'killing time in line' conversation. But as the conversation kept going, I realized I had been set up. God had set me up. But in a good way. I say set up because some of the issues she was describing that she and her fiancee were struggling with were some of the EXACT same issues I had already gone through. So, instead of it being just a random conversation, God gave me a platform to share my testimony with her. And hopefully impart some of God's wisdom allotting for fresh insight in their relationship. So yes, God was using what the enemy thought he was using to shame and guilt me, to be a steppingstone for God to get His Glory. His glory for His forgiveness. His glory for His love. His glory for His mercy. His glory for His grace. God was able to use even me. Only because His Perfect Love loves an imperfectly perfect me.

I have been married for a long time. And yes, there were some unresolved issues in my marriage. But God's grace was giving me a second chance. A second chance to reach back and strengthen my sister who was struggling. A second chance to be able to share with this young woman my experiences on the things NOT to do in marriage. We always share those things we "ought" to do in marriage. But I am here to share the "what-nots" to do in marriage. Those things which may be overlooked. And it is these overlooked things that can fester over time and eventually explode. Those things you take for granted because your partner may be more meek and more humble than you. Those things you become so comfortable with in doing. Even though you know you should not. But, as long as you keep getting away with it, you keep doing it. Ouch. Those things that may seem little to you but are HUGE for your spouse. Those things that you 'sweep under the rug' because they are not as concerning to you as they may be to your spouse. Those behaviors and attitudes you KNOW you should not be displaying to anyone. Let alone your spouse. You know those 'little' things I am talking about, right? You do not have to say them aloud. But you know. This was my lightbulb moment: just because I did not like where I was at in my marriage did NOT give me a pass to be bitter. Because I did not like where I was in my marriage did NOT give me a pass to be spiteful. Because I did not like where I was in my marriage did NOT give me a pass to not STILL give God glory. It was not God's fault that I was where I was in my relationship. God did not do anything to me. God was not punishing me. The devil can make you think so. But God is the exact opposite. Just because your position is not where you want it to be should not smother your praise. Because at the end of the day, God is good ALL the time. And all the time, not some of the time, God IS good! So, I was quickened in my attitude and in my gratitude towards God and I began sowing a seed into this hungry and influential young woman's relationship. At that moment, the outcome of my relationship was not important. But helping this young woman even superseded my own needs and desires. And that is when I understood a little differently. That is when I began to understand Psalm 37:3 so clearly. Trust God and do good. Trust God's Word and do good. Trust and keep sowing. Do not look at your circumstances. Not only trust. But sow into the lives of others. Trust and do good. Trust and do good. That is all that kept looping in my thoughts. And The Holy Spirit kept speaking, reminding me that if I use my testimony, that could be the motivation that could help another couple. Help them not end up in the place where I was at. Even though I did not know the resolve of my own marriage did not mean I should not sow into someone else's marriage to help ensure that they know how to plant "good" seed. You may have heard it before about how you sow where you want to grow? Well, I wanted my own marriage to grow from "good" seed being planted. So that meant I needed to get to planting. And not just planting "random" seeds. But planting intentional seed(s). Planting specific seed(s). Planting definitive seed(s). I needed to start putting a demand on my seed(s) in Jesus' Name.

Was I still a little afraid? Absotively Posilutely. Kind of like calling those things that are not as though they are, huh (Romans 4: 17)? For me, it was almost like telling people you are going to have a baby before you were even pregnant. For me, it was like buying baby items for a baby God promised you. For me, it is like believing against all human intellect and believing for a child when you do not even have a menstrual cycle. Too much? Just know. God will manifest all those things that you have faith to believe for. Just trust Him.

In these next few chapters, you will see me reference, what I call, 'little' charms quite often. For me, these 'little' charms are the scars from all the hurt and pain that I started collecting early on. These 'little' charms became my mask hiding all those bad things that I had gone through in my life. I equated these 'little' charms like the charms on a Pandora bracelet. Pandora bracelets have these definitive little charms that are supposed to give an idea of who you are as a person. Well, all of my 'little' charms were bright, pretty, and all-in place. Yet, that was only a facade. Because each one of them told a story. And the story was not always a good story. These were stories that I had no idea how negatively they had impacted my 'perception' of life. My 'perception' of love. My 'perception' of my reality. And my 'perception' of what I believed to be my truth. All of my 'little' charms, not to brag, but I have single-handedly performed each one first-hand. All of my 'little' charms are all derived from my own personal experiences. However, I need to make you aware of something. These charms are not like the charms on a Pandora bracelet. My 'little' charms were damaged. My 'little' charms' were tarnished. My 'little' charms' were molded. My 'little' charms had mildewed over the years. So much so, that they gave off this awful smelling stinch. But God. God was able to use these same 'little' charms to restore me. God was able to use these same 'little' charms to give me new life. God was able to use these same 'little' charms to polish up my walk with Him. God was able to use these same 'little' charms to heal my brokenness.

Allow me to give this disclaimer. So, please catch it. PSA: I am not a counselor. I am not a therapist. I am not a psychologist. I do not profess to be anything more than what God says I am. And, God says that I am His Child whom He has cleverly disguised as a married woman who is currently separated. I am the mother to a grown son. I am a Pharmacist by trade. And I am also a 'perfectly flawed' sinner whom God has saved by His grace. Read insightfully.

Chapter 1

Life Interrupted

Do you remember a time, period, or even a moment in your life, which altered your course so dratically from what you could have ever imagined? Maybe it was the loss of a close family member and/or friend. Or maybe it was the ending of an old friendship or relationship. Or maybe it was the diagnosis of an unexpected illness. Or maybe it was the closing of a family-owned business that had been around for generations. Whatever that "moment" was for you, can you see how everything changed after getting that news? Can you see how it altered life outside of that you were expecting? Hoping for? Whether you realized it then, or soon after, the bottom line is: if you are here to talk about it, no matter how devastating that season was for you, you made it. Even when you did not think you would make it, you did. Even when the circumstances around you told you that you were not going to make it, you did. Even when you felt like you had one foot in the grave and the other foot was out, you made it. Even when you felt like your heart could not take anymore. You somehow made it. You did it. God did it! The mere fact that you can say "I made it," is a testimony of God's goodness. Whether you realize it or not, God is always mindful of you (Psalm 8:4). The enemy tries to make you fell like God has forgotten about you. But you and I both know that the devil is the father of all liars (John 8:44). So, do not let that seed of doubt get planted in your heart when he tries to convince you that God has forgotten about you. Especially when it does not like your circumstances are changing. God will never forget about His children. Do you not realize how much God loves you? If not, take you pick at reading about the story of Jesus in any one of the gospels ((i.e., Matthew, Mark, Luke, or John). The bible also reminds us in Psalm 37:25, "The righteous have never been forsaken nor his seed begging bread." When you feel like your path is uncertain and your steps aredark, look to His Word (Psalm 119:105). When you feel like you do not know which direction to take, step aside and allow God to order your steps (Psalm 119:133). The one thing the enemy wants to see you achieve at, is being a failure. Failure in your faith. Failure in your relationships. Failure in your life. Failure in God.

So, instead of looking at these times, or seasons, in your life as you are losing something. Or somehow life failing you. How about trying to embrace these times as times of growth. God never wants to take anything from us. He is always looking to get something to us. These times of "stretching" and "pulling" are our opportunities of expansion. Expansion to enlarge our faith in Him. Expansion to enlarge our trust in Him. Expansion to enlarge our territory in Him. Expansion to enlarge our peace in Him. Expansion to enlarge our joy in Him. God is always looking for opportunities to expand us. So, when you feel like you are in a "tight spot" or when life comes at you fast and hard, meditate on James 1:2-3, "Consider it pure joy, my brothers and sisters, whenever you face trials of many kinds, because you know that the testing of your faith produces perseverance." Neither patience nor perseverance is produced overnight. They take time to develop. They take time to cultivate. They take time to mature. But out of these times, you are growing. Growing in faith in God. Growing in trusting God. Just be mindful. It is sometimes DURING these times that things begin to make you feel numb or stagnant in your faith. Just hold on and do not give into your 'feelings.' Wait for it. Wait for it. Wait for it. God WILL show up in your situation. And when He does, He WILL show out. God wants us to understand that EVERYTHING is under His tutelage. God says in Exodus 3:14, "I AM (WHO) I AM." And whatever you need God to be, He says that I AM. God can be anything you need Him to be (Omnipotent). God can be everywhere you need Him to be (Omnipresent). There is nothing that happens that God does not know about. For God knows everything (Omniscient).

Do you remember as kids playing a game called Double Dare? Basically, you would dare someone to do something that either you did not think they would do, or you did not think they could do. Either way, when you got double dared, accepting the dare meant that you were going to 'level up' to the challenge that was presented to you. Well, because how God answered the question about His Identity in Exodus 3:14, only in my mind, I feel like God was saying, "Try Me. I bet I can do it. Give Me a chance to show you how I can 'Level Up'." Being humorous, I feel like sometimes God almost double dares us to try Him. Either way, if we just sit back sometimes and let God be God, He will show us that He's The Master at Double Dare. The Master in the sense that our situation(s) are not there to be the "bigs" in your life. I believe that situations present themselves so that God can show us that He is "bigger" than any "big" we may encounter. We just need to turn the telescope around. And begin to look at our problems from the opposite recommended end. When we shift the telescope around, our problems are so minute compared to the 'infiniteness' and 'bigness' of our God.

Going back to that significant life-altering event that changed your life, just know that God promised that He would never leave nor forsake you (Deuteronomy 31 :6). Bottom line: You cannot get hung up on what you see. For what you see is only temporary. But what God promises us, is eternal (2 Corinthians 4:18). So, no matter what we go through, do not ever think you are going through it by yourself. God never leaves us. For lo, God is with us always, even unto the end of time (Matthew 28:20). Also, if you did not know it then, I am telling you now that God has given us His anointing. An anointing which destroys yokes and removes burdens (Isaiah 10:27). That is the main reason why the enemy fights us so hard. Because he wants us to doubt God's Word. Cause he knows that once our faith mixes with what God tells us, sprinkled with a little anointing on top, we BECOME unstoppable. For all that we go through in life. For all the mountains standing in our way. For every sycamine tree that is resisting getting uprooted, there is only one help. And that one ingredient required to move anything out the way is faith. Faith in God is required for every journey. Faith in God is required for every path. Faith in God is required for every aspect of your life.

Chapter 2

Stay in the Game

F or me, there have been several times throughout my life that have had a great impact to steer me to where I am at this point in my life. Yes, these "life-altering" moments. Take for instance, the months leading up to 2020. These times have been like a "wonder" year for me. So impactful to where the changes in my life had changed my circumstances to greatly that I was forced to incorporate an "adjusted normal" in my way of living. It was in that year that I contemplated quitting my job that I had been working at for over five years. It was in that year that we experienced a different type of financial strain. It was in that year that my husband and I seperated, and my marriage hit those jeopardy waters. It was in that year that I stepped out on faith and decided to take a different career path. It was in that year that our world was stricken with a coronavirus pandemic, Covid-19. And many businesses, including churches, had to shut their doors indefinitely. It was in that year that the Black Lives Matter movement unfotunately became more and more worldwide. It was in that year that we got a new POTUS and the first African American Woman will be sworn in as Vice President. So, the year 2020 has been filled iwth so many "adjusted normals" that we are steadily trying to make the uncomfortable confortable. I am not this faith shero or anything, but I have always tried to carry a little faith in my back pocket. But in the year 2020, this was the season where my faith was put to the test. And hard. I had to put my money where my mouth was. I had to be intentional about totally depending and truting in God for EVERYTHING on a whole new and different level. I had to be intentional about trusting God in my marriage, in my family, in my career, with my mind, with my thoughts, with my finances, with my entire existence. My one assurance was Psalm 139. and although 2020 caught me by surprise, nothing that happens catches God surprise. No matter what was going on arounf me. No matter what I went through. No matter how I sometimes felt like life was tossing me around like a bean bag, God always reminded me that I am never alone. God knew 'life' would happen. He just never intended for us to do it alone. Can I be honest with you? Some days, I honestly did not want to hear that. I wanted the heartache to end. I wanted the pain to stop. I wanted the sleepless nights to be a thing of the past. I wanted my appetite back. I just wanted to smile again. And furthermore, some days I just wanted to mope and grieve for the life that was no longer. I intentionally wanted to wear grave clothes. I intentionally wanted to walk around feeling like I just had the wind knocked out of me. I intentionally wanted to feel sorry for myself. And I wanted to be intentionally felt sorry for. I did not have the mental stability, emotional sincerity, or spiritual genuineness to be concerned about some assignment or what my purpose was. Could God not see that I was losing? Did He not care what was happening in my life and how it was making me so distraught? I did not want to get back on the horse and try again. I just wanted to sit right there in the ditch for a while. Sit right there where the horse threw me off. I was in a dark place. And it did not last only a little while. I made it last a lot longer than what God intended. However, believe it or not, during this time, I was still able to function. I actually felt like a functioning addict, for lack of a better explanation. I had a specific routine I would follow. And little to no times, did I deviate from that. Not because I did not want to at times, but because then that would require me to have to think, feel, or become decisive. With my specific routine, I could do that blind folded. I could do that with ease. I could do that with no missteps. No hesitations. No trouble. And, when things arose outside of that, I often detoured around them because I wanted to stay in that dark place that had become so comfortable and convenient for me. I did not want to talk to people. And I did not. I did not want any help. And I did not ask for any. I did not want to do anything outside of my routine. And over time, I saw myself spiraling. And I knew it because I was beginning to self-medicate. I began drinking more than my usual and more often than I would like to disclose. I was probably going to the liquor store getting my four pack of margaritas maybe twice a week. May not sound like a lot, but for me, it was way too much. You know I was going too often if the clerk knew me by name. And during a quarantine? I was doing the absolute most. But in my mind, when I was not at work, all I wanted to do when I got home was sleep. Sleep away my pain. Sleep away my loneliness. Sleep away my depression. Just sleep. And what better way to sleep than to get tipsy? I say tipsy because I do not like the feeling of a hang.over. So, I knew my limit. I did not consider myself an alcoholic, yet. But I definitely had a different appreciation for those that struggle with this addiction. I did not want to necessarily drink. I just wanted to soothe. I just wanted to numb. I just wanted to forget. In my own little twisted mind, by me drinking, that was my way of holding onto whatever little bit of control I had left in my life.

I cannot say how long I kept up this 'nasty lit· tie habit,' but I can tell you when it slowed down. I was watching a preacher on television one evening. Why? I do not know. I was just channel surfing and I saw this minister. I never actually listened to any of this guy's messages before that night. And the only reason why I actually listened to him was because my husband used to rave about this guy and how good he was. So, why not? I did not have anything more to lose. So, I tuned in. And before I could turn the volume up to a reasonable listening sound, one of the first things I heard him talking about was how someone out there was trying to diminish, or wash, their problems away by drinking. And by how the drinking was only adding on to the problem. Not solving it or resolving it. Just numbing it until you became 'un•numb' again. And then the process would start all over again. I literally dropped the margarita that was in my hand on the floor. I was like, "Okay God. You have got my attention." That night I HEARD God speaking to me. Unlike any of the other times. The preacher was basically preaching about me to me. That was not luck. That was not a coincidence. That was God. And I knew it. And from that day going forward, I vowed to not drown my sorrows in my 'little glass of heaven.' I vowed to not drown my pain in my 'little glass of heaven.' I vowed to not hide my emotions in my 'little glass of heaven.' No matter how hard the next step would be, I was willing to take it. My life depended on it. When I looked around at my life, at myself, I did not recognize me. So, I knew it was time. So, I vowed to confront my issues head on. If I did not know it before, that night I had an encounter with God. God came and sat with me in that dark bedroom and just talked me off the ledge. No one knew how close I was to just letting go and succumbing to my defeat. But God knew. God knew I was 'this' close to jumping. That night in my bedroom, I went to God heartbroken, damaged, broken in spirit, confused, bitter, angry, lonely, depressed, unworthy, anxious, unloved. I went to God a real hot mess! A real basket case. I do not remember how long I prayed or the exact words of my prayer. But I do know that God heard and answered my prayer. It was not, however, a spontaneous "fix." But I did notice that little by little, urges in me began to change. My heart was not as contrite as it had been. Even though I was still living alone, my loneliness was not like it used to be. I was not as depressed as I had been. I found myself being able to interact with people sincerely and compassionately. I noticed that I was beginning to learn how to laugh a little more. I noticed my desire and quench for life was being restored. I was slowly able to begin enjoying life. This may sound crazy. But it is my truth. Even though I was in a dark place, it did not stop God from blessing me. Even when I was not grateful. Even when I did not acknowledge His goodness. Even when I allowed other things to overshadow my praise. God never skipped a beat. God did not stop loving me because of my situation. God did not stop loving me because of my mistakes. God did not stop loving me because of my bad choices. God's grace never stopped flowing in my life. It was like God gave me a 'make-over' and I began to have a different outlook on life. A different outlook on myself. A different outlook on my circumstances. I was beginning to enjoy the blessings God had poured on me even while in the midst of this pandemic of COVID-19. I was beginning to have a new appreciation for the time being spent with my family. I began to have a different appreciation for the new job that God had blessed me with. And this job was opening doors for new opportunities in growth, creativity, and expansion. I experienced a different pleasure in hearing, listening, and writing what the Holy Spirit led me to write. This may sound funny, but I was actually able to look in my mirror and like what was staring back at me. I actually began to like being in my own company.

With all that was going on around me. With all that I was allowing to keep my focus. With all that I was allowing to distract me, I had lost sight of God. COVID-19 had not stopped God's rain of favor from showering down on me. God closing one door of employment did not stop God from opening up another door for me. God was still faithful even though I had been living in the valley of the shadows of death. He did not leave me there. God's grace and mercy picked me up and reminded me Whose daughter I was. And God said that I was worthy. Not because I was married. Not because I was a mother. Not because I was a Pharmacist. Not because I was a daughter. Not because I was a sister, a friend, a neighbor, or even a co-worker. All those titles did not qualify me for God's grace. Actually, none of those titles qualified me for God's grace. God qualified me simply because He loves me. And God was consistently showing me that I was worthy just because He said I was. God knew where I would be and the specific time of the day I would be there. And guess what? He had already made provisions for me to come out. He had already made provisions to meet me there. He promised to give me this day my daily bread (Matthew 6:11). All I had to do was ask and believe that He would provide. So, asking for His peace, became my routine. Asking for His provisions, became my routine. Asking for His guidance, became my routine. Asking for His joy, became my routine. Asking for His wisdom, became my routine. Asking for His Will over my life, became my routine. I would also like to add that it was also during this time, that God reminded me that just because I had gone through some life altering changes. And even though my "sweeping things under the rug" way of life had proven to be more detrimental than beneficial. And even though my circumstances had changed, did not mean that God's purpose for my life had changed. My purpose was the same regardless of where I was or what was going on. My purpose was the same regardless of if I even acknowledged it or not. So, the sooner I came to that understanding within myself, the sooner God could really begin to start using me. Using my struggles to testify of His goodness. Using my struggles to help life someone else. Using my struggles to keep me humble. Knowing that if it were not for God's grace, I would not be where I am today.

For some, the year 2020 will be just a remembrance of the "adjusted normals" we have all had to implement. However, for me, the year 2020 was my rebirth year. My second chance year. My year that God called me to the carpet. My year to lay to rest the old version of who I used to be. My year to lay to rest the old version of what I used to be. My year to lay to rest the old version of "Me." And, my year to finally meet the 'New and Restored' Tena. So, no matter what life holds for you, always remember that you are not what you have been through. There is only one name you answer to and that's Child of God. And of course, your government name. Basically, do not let your circumstances dictate your destiny. Jeremiah 1:5 states, "Before I formed you in the womb, I knew you. Before you were born, I set you apart." You have been purposed for a time such as this. Things may not happen in your timing. But it will happen in God's timing. You just have to trust His timing. You have a special quality about you. And with God's strength lifting you up when you are weak, you will persevere through. Remember, with God, all things are possible (Matthew 19:26). So, do not count yourself out too quickly.

If you know like I know, God is a God of second chances. After second chance. After second chance. And then a second chance all over again. If a righteous man falls seven times (Proverbs 24:16), what makes you think you are not going to fall? Newsflash: YOU ARE. Just do not stay there. Get up. Pick yourself up. Dust your knees off. Pick your head up. Straighten up your shoulders. And put one foot in front of the other and walk by faith one step-at-a-time. You are not defeated. You just got knocked down. So, gather your composure and get back in the race. God sees your efforts. God sees your heart. So, in everything you do, do it by faith. Trust me, God will meet you where you are at. He loves you. You are the apple of His eye. Life will come with challenges. Life will come with struggles. But know this, no matter what kind of obstacles life throws at you. No matter how many obstacles try to get in your way. No matter how many mountains try to block what God has for you, stand on The Word. We may fail The Word, but The Word never fails us. Stay your course. Stay in your lane. Stay in your assignment. And watch God "stand up" flooded Jordan wates to allow you to safely pass through (Joshua 3:8-17). Selah.

Chapter 3

Straighten Up…

While in prayer one morning, God revealed something to me that blew my mind. I am sure that I have mentioned before that me and my husband are separated. And we have been for some time now. But while praying, God told me that the same way I am physically estranged from my husband, that I had become spiritually estranged from Him. And I had been for a while. At first, I did not understand. But when God gives you clarification, you had better be lying prostrate. Because God showed me, "Me." First off, allow me to explain exactly what this word means. Just so we can make sure that we are on the same page. To be estranged means to no longer be close or affectionate towards a person. It means to become alienated. God told me that even though my husband and I had been living in the same house, we had become estranged. Yes, my husband and I had been lying next to each other in the same bed. Yet, we had become estranged. There was a distance that had grown in between us that had caused us to become estranged. And when God told me that 'our' re-lationship had also become estranged the same way as well. And, as long as I was estranged from God, everything else around me will be es-tranged and disconnected as well. My marriage. My job. My relationships. My health. My mind. My thoughts. My finances. Now, please do not get it twisted. God CAN is ABLE to do anything. But until I got things into proper alignment, into God's proper order, estrangement would continue to be my residence.

Just like in life, the alignment process is never comfortable. But it is necessary. If you could just withstand the process and trust God through the process, the end result will be worth it. The alignment process will be but a memory. Allow me to share my testimony. When I first got braces as a young teen, I had to first get spacers in between my teeth. And that was only the beginning. I then had to get some teeth extracted here and there. And thus, the beginning phases of the alignment process were on the horizon. They had to do all this work before they were even able to put the braces on. What they were ultimately doing was trying to make room for what they were planning. They were trying to make room for what they had purposed. They were trying to make room for what was about to come. They were trying to prepare for the overall outcome. They had to remove some things here and shift some things around there in order to make room for the expected end. And just like in God's alignment process, sometimes some things have to be removed from here and some other things shifted around over there, in order to make room for what He has in store for you. But know this, whatever God removes, He is able to replace double fold over. I get it. Nobody likes the process. But everyone sure loves the results. However, after the alignment process was over and I was able to actually SEE the manifested results of my process, I forgot all about how difficult the process was. I loved my teeth. I loved my smile. I looked at myself in the mirror and I had seen someone I had never seen before. I had a confidence that was brand new. So much so, that I could not stop smiling. And my smile has become like my 'signature' trademark; even now. This is how the alignment process with God is. It is by no means comfortable. But if you can hold on through the process to get to the end, you almost forgot about the extracting pain, the tightening and squeezing, and the feeling like your teeth are about to fall out of your mouth. The results truly outweigh the process. You forget about what you had to lose in order to gain. You forgot about what you had to go through in the beginning. Because all you see staring back at you is a confident, bold, faith-filled little girl that you did not even know existed. And it is like I was meeting her for the very first time.

I remember one evening, when I was like 7 or 8 years old, my grandmother's best friend asked me a strange question. She asked me if I was unhappy because she rarely saw me smile. I did not realize that I hardly smiled. I guess I was just comfortable being uncomfortable. That is, until someone pointed it out. Being so young, I was not aware that I was wearing my insecurities on my sleeve. I was not aware that my vulnerabilities were showing up on the outside. I can admit. I did not have the prettiest of smiles. Because truth be told, my teeth were jacked up. Outside of getting my fluent flow of sarcasm from my father, I also got his small jawline packed with a million itty bitty teeth. And all these itty-bitty teeth were crooked and stacked on top of one another. And just to add a little more lagniappe, I was also vertically challenged and a little on the chubby side. So, no. I never felt pretty. Plus, my hair had fallen out from a bad relaxer I had gotten. My self-esteem was jacked up. What I did not know was that the evidence of how I was feeling on the inside was showing up on the outside. And, since I am on a roll. I believe, in my heart of hearts, that all these insecurities wrapped up in one big ball, made it easy for my molester to begin their reign of terror. My molester saw my weaknesses. My molester played on my vulnerabilities. My molester took advantage of my insecurities. My molester knew that I just wanted to be loved and made to 'feel' like I was pretty. My molester knew that I was craving attention. And in their sick mind, they gave it to me. Did you know that molestation is never about 'the act?' It is always about the manipulation behind the act. It is about the power and the intimidation behind the act. It is almost never about the act itself. It is just a sick and twisted game. Mind games. When a person touches a child inappropriately, they are sick. They have an illness. Because nowhere in a person's mind should there be a 'green light' to violate a child. A child that you are supposed to love. A child that you are supposed to protect. A child that you are supposed to comfort and nurture. A child that believes they can trust you. It took me a long time to not only forgive my molester. But to also forgive them. I knew I had to because forgiveness was not about them. Forgiveness was about me. And not let hatred get buried in my heart. And not let bitterness get buried in my heart. And not let a wall get built around my heart. Can I be honest? I forgave my molester years ago. But I never dealt with the effects of what had happened to me. I never dealt with the unresolved effects of how I felt when all this was going on. I never dealt with any of it. And to be quite honest, it ended up dealing with me. I say the effects dealt with me because the 'not talking about' my trauma ended up surfacing in my marriage, at all the wrong times. The effects showed up without any warning. They showed up without any invitation. And when they did show up, they had the nerve to not even be hospitable. They actually showed up rudely!

When I really understood how God is align ing things in my life, to make the pieces fit, tears just streamed down my face. Even if that means that sometimes I have to be uncomfortable in order to get to the place where God wants me, my heart was full. Even if that means weeping may endure for a night. I know joy. God's joy will come in the morning (Psalm 30:5). Even if that means that my life looks like it is going haywire, I know that God is working all things together for my 'good' because I love Him and have been called according to His purpose (Romans 8:28). So, my prayer life changed. My prayers became a prayer of praise. A praise to God for getting things into alignment in my life. A praise to God for getting things into align ment in my health. A praise to God for getting things into align ment in my finances. A praise to God for getting things into alignment with my child. A praise to God for getting things into alignment in my marriage. Regardless of what my life consisted of, if I was not willing to put, and keep, God first, then things would always be out of alignment.

Then, every single aspect of my life and my relationships would all be in a state of estrangement. And the way that God wanted to align things in my life is to make Him my foundation. If I did not get things in its proper order, it would be like I was being foolish and building on sinking sand (Matthew 7:24-27). Everything would continue to crumble. Everything would continue to shatter. Everything would continue to produce cracks.

Then He could begin to align everything else around me. God first had to align my heart to His. I had to desire to seek after His Kingdom first (Matthew 6:33). This was my responsibility first. And sometimes, we can get hung up on how God wants to bless us. And yes. God does desire to bless His children. But there is always a prerequisite first. And this prerequisite typically involves some act of faith. And if faith is not your thing, I get it, seeking the kingdom somewhat farfetched. But try to think about it this way. I think you need to understand that WE are the kingdom. You ARE the kingdom. I AM the kingdom. Adhering to God's Will and His Ways on the inside of you are The Kingdom. Some folks think the kingdom is the church. The church is the church. That is the structure where all the 'kingdom builders' meet. If the church, however, is the kingdom, then we are in a bit of a pickle. Considering the pandemic state, the world is in right now. Some churches have closed their doors for good. A lot of churches are still not able to congregate because of COVID-19. So, if that is the only place where you can find the kingdom, then we are in a definite bind. The Kingdom starts from within us. From the God within us. God put His Kingdom on the inside of me and you. And if I do not seek God first and what He put on the inside of me (Le., the seed from Matthew 13:24-30), and align my will and my way unto His first, then EVERYTHING else around me will be added. Everything else around me will come into alignment as well. God's alignment. And for me, the bottom line is if I am outside of God's alignment, I am not living. If I am outside of God's alignment, I do not even exist. If I am outside of God's alignment, nothing around me can be rebuilt. So, God, I give you permission to align my heart to Yours. God, I give you permission to align my will to Yours. God, I give you permission to align my ways to Yours. God, I give you permission to align my life to Yours. I cannot be estranged from you any longer. God, You are my lifeline and I trust you to align things in my life so our relationship can be what You have always desired it to be.

Chapter 4

What-Nots #1

Nothing Comes Before God ...

B eing married for over 17 years, I was fortunate enough to meet so many of my husband's family. Outside of his immediate family, I had the privilege and honor to meet his great grandmother very early in our relationship. She was this beautiful, savvy, and very witty seasoned Christian woman, who could put together a meal with two fish and five loaves of bread. Upon meeting her, I immediately adopted her as my great grandmother as well I can remember going to her home with my husband just talking or eating dinner after church on Sundays. Outside of her anointed hands in the kitchen' she had this collection which displayed things called "what-nots." A "what-not" is used to refer to an item or items that are not identified but are felt to have something in common with items already named. Mama Nea, as I will call her, had so many of these different porcelain figurine types all over. Upon seeing them, it brought back such childhood memories of when I used to visit my great aunt. So, immediately, I knew exactly what they were when I first saw them. I remember just wanting to hold them and just admire the unique and specific details of each one. But I restrained myself because they can be quite delicate. Each of these "what-nots" carry their own unique "flare." These small little "what-nots" hold so much meticulous beauty. They look so priceless and fragile. Yet, because of their material, they are actually quite sturdy. As I was just sitting one day, just meditating on nothing in particular, Mama Nea's collection of what-nots dropped in my spirit. And then the Holy Spirit began revealing some things to me. I was told that we, as people, are like "what-nots." When God created us, He created us so unique and distinctly specific that there is absolutely no one else in the world quite like you. We each have our own distinct specificities. We each have our own detailed design. We were created to be Tonka tough. Yet, we can be flexible and resilient under certain conditions. God put His hand-made seal on each of us that has made us authentically authentic. When God created us, He gave us the strength to be able to move mountains (Matthew 17:20) and withstand fires (Daniel 3:19-25). God said that everything He created was good (1 Timothy 4:4). God said that we are wondefully made (Psalm 139:14). God said that we are His Masterpieces (Ephesians 2:10). God has put His Own DNA in us (Genesis 1:27).

Sometimes we may feel weak, frail or even delicate. Sometimes we may look like we are going to 'break' in the midst of chaos. But rest assured, God made us sturdy. Everything that we need to overcome, God has already equipped us with (2 Peter 1:3). In life, we will get some scratches or bruises here and there. We may experience some 'wear and tear' every now and then. But remember, sometimes it is the things that look the weakest that prove to be the strongest. Never underestimate. You never know the durability of something until it has been tested. You never know the durability of something until it is ripped. You never know the durability of something until it has slipped and fell. You never know the durability of something until it has been dropped. You have durability. You have strength. God's strength is our resilience. Our resilience of what is not going to happen. Our resilience of what we are not going to accept. Our resilience of what is not going to defeat us. Just as the potter carved and molded each and every precious and unique "what-nots," is the same way that our Potter (i.e., God) has carved and molded us (i.e., clay) in His strong hands (Isaiah 64:8).

This may sound crazy, but I have come to give my scars, my life-altering scars, names. I give them names because at one point in time, we were very intimate. At one point in time, I went to bed with them and I woke up with them. At some point in time, we ate dinner and had a Netflix and chilled kind of evening. At some point in time, they were my confidant. At some point in time, we were each other's backbone and sounding board. At some point in time, I let their identity become my identity. At some point in time, we had become so intertwined that I did not know where my scar ended, and I began. At some point in time, I yielded and made us matching BFF bracelets. I do not know how or when 'it' happened, but I no longer saw me. All I saw was what I had been through. But then one day, something happened. Something in me changed. My attitude changed. My mindset changed. Something in me wanted something different. Something in me got tired of this relationship. Please let me say this. I am not ashamed of my scars because they tell my story. I am not ashamed because my story does not end there. I realized that there is more to me than the scars that were left as a result of trauma. There was more to me than the scars that were left as a result of pain. There was more to me than scars that were left as a result of bullying. There was more to me than scars that were left as a result of molestation. There was more to me than scars that were left as a result of Daddy issues. There was more to me than the scars that were left as a result of insecurities. There was more to me than the scars that were left as a result of vulnerabilities There was more to me than the scars that were left as a result of mistakes. It was time to regain the identity that I had lost. It was time to regain the identity of how God sees me. And here is just a bit of that conversation that God and I had about this. God told me, "As long as 'You' do not know who you are and what is on the inside of you, you will continue to be unsteady. I put a 'what-not' spirit on the inside of you. A spirit of 'what I am not willing to accept.' I put a 'fighting' spirit on the inside of you. I put a 'praying' spirit on the inside of you. I put an 'anointed' spirit on the inside of you. I put a 'winning' spirit on the inside of you. There are things in life that you should just not accept. But until you realize that you are 'My' daughter, you will forever be forfeiting the benefits of your inheritance." After hearing this, I can admit, I was humbled. Humbled because I never considered myself to have any of those characteristics that God told me I had. I was always this 'background' type of person. But God said that I was a fighter? A prayer warrior? Anointed? A winner? My circumstances told me that I was not any of those things. My circumstances told me that I was just the opposite of everything God had just told me. But God. Before I allowed God's Word to get snatched by the enemy, God put a song in my spirit. I did not even know the actual name or the artist. I was just given a few words. Thank goodness for phone apps because that is right where I went to. I later found out that the song was actually by one of my favorite artists. This was a song by Tasha Cobbs Leonard, and it was a song off her latest album: Heart. Passion. Pursuit. The song is called, "Forever at Your Feet." And while I was listening to the song, when I heard it, I knew this was the message God was trying to imprint in my spirit. In my heart. The lyrics are really simple. Yet, they are so prophetic. It is a little medley that says, "I'll be seated at Your feet. To worship at Your feet. I'll be right here at Your feet, forever." And in that moment, God spoke to me and He reminded me of my place. God told me that whenever I am out of alignment from where He has placed me, I will always 'feel' out of order. My position in Him is a position of worship. My seat in Him is a position of worship. My posture in Him is a position of worship. And it is in this place of worship where God's peace is at. It is in the sacredness of worship where God's rest is at. It is in the sacredness of worship where God's joy is at. It is in the sacredness of worship where God's wisdom is at. It is in the sacredness of worship where God's authority is at. And, when I am out of my seat in Him, I am out of my position. My God-given position is in His presence. Being in God's presence opens your Heart for worship with Him. Being in God's presence stirs up a Passion for worship with Him. Being in God's presence ignites a Pursuit in you to want to chase after God and His Righteousness. A special place of worship in Him. And when I am out of my ordained position of authority, the enemy wants me to worry. Worry about my circumstance. Worry about my health. Worry about my finances. Worry about my family. Worry about this pandemic. Worry about my job. Worry about things I have lost. Worry about my child. Worry about my life. Worry about my marriage. Worry about everything. The enemy tries to be so cunning. But he is such a liar. The one thing I have learned this past year is that whenever your warfare is great, the enemy knows that your destiny is great. Because the enemy would not be fighting you so hard if he did not think your purpose was bigger than where you are at right now. You obviously got something to add to The Kingdom. You obviously got something that is going to give God's Name the glory. You obviously got something that is going to strengthen your brother or sister as they are going through. Girlllllll, you must have something great on the inside of you!

Getting back to when the Holy Spirit gave me this illustration about Mama Nea's "what-nots," my heart skipped a beat. Like really. And it just was not my heart murmur. LOL. Because everyone can always tell you how to do this or how to do that. But I was told to forewarn on things not to do in order to prevent an outcome that you do not want to have to deal with.

This was my testimony! For these little "whatnots" should help explain those things of what not to do in order to stay in proper alignment with God. They will hopefully help explain those things of what not to do in order to stay in proper order with God. They will hopefully help explain those things of what not to do in order to stay in proper posture with God. They will hopefully help explain those things of what not to do to make all of your pieces fit. I may not be able to tell you how to be this or how to be that. But I sure can tell you 'what not' to do or 'what not' to say or how not to behave. Unfortunately, over the years, I became an expert in this area. However, it is these exact "what-nots" that I am hoping will help you not make some of the same mistakes that I made. It is these exact same "what-nots" that can keep you distant from God's good graces. It is these exact same "what-nots" that can deceive and blind you from desiring to please God. It is these exact same "what-nots" that will fool you into thinking you do not need God. It is these exact same "whatnots" that the enemy tries to keep us in bondage with. It is these exact same "what-nots" that can ultimately lead you into living a defeated life. A defeated life in your relationships. A defeated life in your marriage. Do you understand now how "what-nots" are equivalent to your strong-holds? These are what the enemy can use to keep you in condemnation and prevent you from walking with God and wanting to be closer to Him. These are what the enemy can use to keep you from wanting to be more intimate with God. These are what the enemy can use to keep you from wanting to be in relationship with God. The "whatnots" are the subtle tricks the enemy uses to keep us in guilt. Shame. Embarrassment. Feeling hypocritical. Sin. The lesson of "what-nots" is to draw you in a closer relationship with God and not fall for the okie doke. And if I was chosen to be the example, "Here I am."

Once you are postured in the right position with God, He will position you in all of your other aspects of your life (Matthew 6:33). But you have to put God in position first. God used something natural and practical to demonstration how He has always desired to position my life. Truthfully, I would much rather be sharing my experiences of what I did 'right' versus sharing my experiences of what I did not do right. Having God give me this revelation of "whatnots," I am hoping will help you.

There is this Dove commercial that I love. In the commercial, they are showing all different types of women testing out their product. Women of all different ethnicities. Women with all different body shapes. Women of all different ages. Women with skin deformities. And yes, even women with visible scars. It is an absolutely beautiful commercial. Then the Holy Spirit whispered so softly to me, "I made you. Love the skin you are in. Embrace every wrinkle. Caress every scar. Squeeze every curve. Nurture every mole. I do not make mistakes. Just love the skin you are in." So, this is my soapbox moment: I love my skin! All this skin that has been abused. All this skin that has been battered. All this skin that has been bruised. All this skin that has been stretched out. All this skin that has endured scars. And yes, even my self-inflicted scars. Everything about me, tells a story. My scars tell my story. But I will not let them stop my purpose. My scars show my insecurities. But I will not let them stop my destiny. My scars tell of my vulnerabilities. But I will not let them define my existence. My scars have a name. But I will not allow them to influence me to answer to what I went through. My scars have left me broken. But I will not let them silence my testimony. From this day forward, declare this with me, "I am CHOOSING to love the skin I am in, in Jesus Name!

Chapter 5

It's Cold on the Porch...

Have you heard the saying, "You can't teach an old dog new tricks?" Would you agree or disagree? If I would have been asked this question years ago, the "old" me probably would have agreed; more or less. But Thank God for fresh revelations. Because the "new" me today, wholeheartedly disagrees with this statement. Want to know why? Because guess what, I am that old dog! Allow me to explain. I was raised by very head-strong and opinionated men and women. And I say this next statement very tastefully and respectfully. But they often believed that their way was sometimes the best way. At times, the only way. So, you can imagine the mindset that helped shape the world of an impressionable young girl. Girl, someone could be wrong as two left feet, I would be shocked if they admitted it. I may be exaggerating a bit. But my family is just cut from a unique cloth. Not easily swayed. Not easily compromising. Not easily convinced. But what happens when what you are standing for is only right for you? What happens when what you are standing for negatively affects someone else? What happens when what you are standing for has no long-term benefit? At what point do you compromise? At what point do you bend to the concerns or ideas of others? At what time do you take the time to listen? Not just hear. But actually listen. At what point in time will you just remain that old dog that is reluctant to learning new tricks? Reluctant to learn new tricks of compromising. Hesitant to learn new tricks of giving. Innovative ways to learn new tricks of communicating. Productive ways to learn new tricks of resolving conflict. Creative ways to learn new tricks of compassion. Imaginative ways to learn new tricks of intimacy. Seductive ways to learn new adventures of love. At some point in any relationship, and in your marriage, you will have to decide what is more important to you:

being right or "acquiring" some new tricks. I am hoping your answer was the latter for $300 Alex. But if it was not. When you get to the point where you stop learning, then you have gotten to the point where you will stop growing. And you won't have anyone to blame but your 'too cute' self.

Remember when I said that I was that old dog? Well, here is the 'real' reason why I said that. My confession moment. Sometimes it takes lifealtering consequences to open your eyes to the error of your ways. For me, that life-altering consequence was my physical and emotional separation from my husband. And it was not until this old dog got 'put off' the porch that I realized that something was really wrong in my marriage. Just like your own dog may be confused as to why they cannot come back inside after making a mess or having an accident inside the house. Well, it was no different for me. And for a while, I did not understand why the screen door, or the wooden door never would open. For a while, I did not understand why my water and food bowls were no longer on the porch. For a while, I did not understand why I could not get my favorite blanket or chew toy. For a while, I did not understand why I was not getting petted and pampered like I used to get. After a while, when I was not getting checked on anymore, that is when I KNEW I was really confined to living only in the doghouse. The only thing was that my doghouse was in a whole different city, close to 2 hours away. Please do not take any of this literally. God just gives me practical life analogies to speak to me. This is only an analogy. Just follow along with the demonstration and you will see where I am going. Just stay open-minded.

I cannot say how many nights it took or how many different seasons I went through, but eventually, I stopped waiting for the porch light to come on and the front door to open. The front door that I have never gotten locked out of before. The front door that used to be so welcoming and inviting. The front door that used to be my place of refuge. The front door that used to be my security. So, as I sat outside just watching the front door, waiting for any sign of activity, I began to grow weary. Grew weary anticipating. Grew weary expecting. Grew weary hoping. Grew weary physically. Grew weary emotionally. Grew weary spiritually. Just weary and exhausted in every sense of the word. And just when I thought I was at my lowest point, and could not get any lower, God threw me a life preserver. God sent me a Word. As I was casually texting my friend one day, she sent me this long, drawn out text message. You see, nine out of ten times, I was too embarrassed to share with anyone how I was REALLY feeling. So, I did not. I kept everything to myself. I did not talk. I did not confide. I did not share. I did not do any of that. However, this text I received; I knew God was reaching out to me. I knew that God was trying to get my attention. And, in a nutshell, God asked me one question, "Am I not enough?" My heart sank when I read it because I knew exactly what it meant. She may not have known what it was she was sending me. But I knew. You see, I had been so preoccupied about getting back on the porch and eventually getting welcomed back inside the house, that those were the thoughts that predominantly consumed my mind. And no matter how hard I tried to focus on other things, my thoughts were winning that fight. These thoughts, I am a little embarrassed to admit, had become like an 'idol' god to me. An idol god because I was giving and feeding them so much attention and they became my desire. They became my intention. They became my determination. And if you did not know, not only was I in error, but I was breaking two of The Ten Commandments; I knew right off the back. First commandment being the very 1st one, "You shall have no other gods before me (Exodus 20:3)." And 'gods' can be interpreted as anything that you worship over God, our Heavenly Father. Unbeknownst to me, I was making my thoughts my god. I was making my feelings my god. I was subconsciously making my desires to "get back in good graces" with my husband my god. The second commandment I was in error behind was, drumroll please, you got it! The very next commandment. The second commandment. And it says, "You shall not make for yourself an image in the form of anything in heaven above or on the earth beneath or in the waters below. You shall not bow down to them or worship them; for I, the Lord your God, am a

41

jealous God (Exodus 20:4-5)." Again, and it goes without saying that I was making my husband, the man himself, my god. Again, I was giving God room to be jealous because of all the "things" I was using to replace Him. So, when God used my friend to text me this message, I was immediately stopped dead in my tracks. She literally had no idea some of the persuasions I was thinking about, to try and get off that porch. She literally had no idea some of the ideas I was conjuring up, to try and get off that porch. She literally had no idea the low points in my mind, where I had been residing, when she texted me. I could hide my thoughts and even my feelings from everyone else. But I could not hide it from God. He knew. And that day, I was getting called to the carpet. Walking in shame. All I could do was repent. I knew what I was doing. But I really did not KNOW what I was doing. However, considering that God was even merciful enough to try and get my attention, I knew some things had to be different going forward. God was giving me another second chance. I was so humbled and grateful that God even took the time to get a message to me. Who am I that God is even mindful of me (Psalm 8:4)? Who am I that God even knows my name (Isaiah 43:1)? Then God told me that I Am His Masterpiece (Ephesians 2: 10). Yes, I may have some little "charms." Yes, I may have some misguided perceptions. Yes, I may have compartmentalized and guarded my heart. But even regardless of all that, there is no one like me. When God made me, He broke the mold. In my mind, and only in my mind, when God finished making me, He dropped the mic! Yes, I am perfectly flawed. But with God's grace, I am continuing to become all that He says I am.

In that one little question God asked me, I believe God was trying to teach me those things of what not to do. And not just things NOT TO DO in marriage. But things not to do in my relationships. Things not to do in my life. God was trying to streamline my life, my will, to His. When I really started to live my life in a manner which pleases God, that is when the rules of the game changed. God was giving me my own little version of "what-nots." These are "what-nots" of the things I should not be saying. These are "what-nots" of the things that do not honor Him. These are "what-nots" of things that do not align to His Word. These are "what-nots" of things that quiet your praise. These are "what-nots" of things that do not give God glory. So, my very first "what-nots" was actually based from Exodus 20:3. There is nothing or no one that should become before God. Not myself. Not my spouse. Not my child. Not my parents. Not my job. Not my finances. Nothing can or should take the place of The One True and Living God. Because if you did not know it, God IS a jealous God. If you think I am exaggerating, read Exodus 20:4. Not only does God tell you NOT to put ANYTHING before Him in verse 3, but verse also 4 tells you what will happen if you do. Read it for yourself. Now, back to our regularly scheduled program.

So, here I was, so driven and head-strong about getting back on that porch, that I was losing sight of everything else around me. That 'porch' became my focus. That 'porch' became my passion. That desire became my sin. Well, one of them anyway. I was losing sight of God. Sidebar: during my separation, God was continually showing Himself strong. Just not in the areas where I would have liked Him to be moving. God was showing Himself in other areas. I was just ignoring God and being selfish. Just wanting what I wanted when I wanted it. I was so blinded because all I had was "marriage on the brain" twenty-four-seven. Not that having the concerns of my marriage was a sin. But making it my world was the sin. Because like I previously stated, it can become more than a forethought. It had become my pre-thought. My mid-day thought. My evening thought. My late night thought. Any way you can think of a thought, IT had become that. And because of it, I was 'missing' God. I was 'dismissing' God. I was 'ignoring' God. I was putting God on the backburner. I was down-playing God. Prime example. During this season of my separation, I was blessed to start a brand-new job as the Pharmacy Manager of an independent pharmacy. I was blessed to get a brand-new luxury car with only 4 miles on it. I was blessed to live in a beautiful penthouse-type apartment with 15-foot ceilings. I was blessed to be able to "splurge" shopping whenever I wanted to. And all this, all these luxuries, on a salary much less than I was accustomed to making. God was moving things around in my life so evidently that I knew it could not be nobody but God doing it. God was removing me from this place. God was placing me in that place. God was opening doors that I was not expecting or even looking for to be opened. God was ministering to me through writing. God was humbling and preparing me for this enormous assignment that frightened the bejeebers out of me. God was definitely moving. I just was not satisfied because it was not in the area of my marriage. Ungrateful. Trust me, I know. And, I have repented. Oh, and let me also say, that it was also during this time of being 'off the porch,' that I was able to confront, process, own, and deal with some deep-rooted childhood issues that had been affecting my decisions and choices thus far. Please do not take this the wrong way because you know how bad I wanted to get off that porch. But, if I had never been put on the porch in the first place, I do not believe that I would be where I am today in my walk with God. It took some very drastic and painful measures to occur, but I believe in my heart of hearts that God was trying to do a new thing in my life. And I had been missing it because I was putting other 'gods' in His place. And I am not just talking about my marriage. But I am talking about the choices I had been making in my life as a whole. But, when God asked me that question, "Am I not enough," I knew things in my life had to change. It was time to stop playing 'church' and acting 'churchy.' It was time to start living, breathing, and having a 'real' relationship with God. So, I HAD to make a choice. I HAD to decide what was going to get my attention. I HAD to decide what was most important to me. Because honestly, I had only been giving God a little bit of wiggle room to work in my life. And I designated the area where I wanted the wiggle room to occur. I know. So sad. But God. Because, it was in this little wiggle room, where I received God's grace. It was in this little wiggle room where I received God's mercy. It was in this little wiggle room that God reminded me of His "what-nots."

So, just to reiterate my answer to the previous question. I can boldly answer now that I believe you can teach an old dog new tricks because God is teaching me. Instead of allowing the "old" me to take the reins, the "new" me has given God that position. Instead of walking out my will and way for my life, God is in His Rightful Place. Instead of always trying to be in control, God has gladly taken over that position as well. And it is in our intimate meditation time, that He is healing me through His Word. It is in our intimate meditation time that God is restoring through His grace. It is in our intimate meditation time that God is reminding me how much He loves me. It is also in our intimate meditation time that God is training me through my own little personal "what-nots." Since there is no respect of persons with God (Romans 2:11), the teaching, the compassion, the grace, and the healing that He has done, and is still doing for me, He CAN do for you. The question is, "Will you let Him?"

Chapter 6

What-Nots #2

Learn to Follow Before Leading...

For this next part, please do not shoot the messenger. If you would just receive the message with your heart and not just your ears, I promise the message will bless you because it is not my own. I am going to present this to you just how it was presented to me. No more. No less. Ready? Dogs have tails and need to be told what to do. Your spouse does not. Mules need to be led by bit and bridle (Psalm 32:9). Your spouse does not. Babies need to be diapered and burped. Your spouse does not. We all have a role to play. I know I have gone from one extreme to the other. But we all have a position we should contribute to the team. The quarterback may not necessarily try to block on the defensive line. The tight end may not necessarily kick the winning punt. The referee may not necessarily walk off the field and start initiating plays from the sidelines. Sounds weird I know. But bottom line, everyone has a part to play. A specific role. A unique role that only they can add to the team. As long as you play your position. As long as you give it all you got. As long as you stay in shape. And always be willing to train to be better at your position. What am I saying? Know your position. Know your role. Train to always be better. Train to always be the best at your role. You be the MVP at your game. So, stop treating your spouse like you need to raise him. Stop treating your spouse like you need to discipline them like what you think they should have gotten as a child. Stop talking to your spouse like they are one of the children. Truth be told. If you feel like you have to do any of these things, the problem is not with them. Maybe you need to look in the mirror. It is not them that need to be corrected. It just maybe you. If you are always trying to change someone into what you think they should be, it is not them that needs changing. You need to take a hard look at yourself. And trust me, seeing fault within yourself, can be a hard job. If you have to change a person to try to make them fit into the mold you think they ought to fit into, that is not their issue, that is yours. That is why it is so important to know yourself, the 'real' you.

Now, I understand we will all have some baggage. And some of that baggage we may not know we are even carrying. But it is unfair to allow your baggage to become someone else's baggage. It is unfair to allow your insecurities to become someone else's insecurities. It is unfair to allow your defeats to become someone else's defeats. A lot of times, if you are so busy trying to correct or change someone, it is because you are trying to avoid addressing the many issues you may be hiding. You "growing up" your spouse is not what marriage should be all about.

To everything under the sun, there is an order. For example, you do not see birds giving birth to fish or cows mating with eagles. And because this order is God-ordained, God blesses this order (1 Corinthians 14:33). Now, this order will only work if the house, and its contents (i.e., the people) belong to God. Just as is stated in Matthew 12:25, "A house divided against itself will not stand (Matthew 12:25)." Everyone has to be on one accord. Everyone in the house has to maintain their position. Everyone in the house has to maintain their role. Everyone in the house must continue with their contribution. In Genesis 1:27, God created man in His own image, first. It was later in Genesis 2:22, that 'wo-man' was later created from the image of man. Man's purpose is designed to be the head of the house. To have dominion (Genesis 1:28). Man is the one who has to answer to God for the accountability of the house. You will notice in Genesis 3:9, although Eve was the one who disobeyed, and succumbed to temptation in The Garden of Eden, when God found out about her disobedience, He did not go to Eve first. God called out straight for Adam. God commands order. God ordains order. God promotes order. I understand there may be a few that may not necessarily agree with me. I get it and I will proceed on. Just allow me to continue. Remember, listen with your heart and not your ears.

A lot of households may not have a man who is redeeming their role as the head and a lot of women have had to 'level up' and subsequently play more than their fair share of roles. Whether your particular situation is by choice or by circumstance, I am not here to debate or even address that. For the mere sake of argument, let us just say all things are equal. We are all playing on a level playing field. And as tactfully and respectively as I want this to come across, I do not want us to miss the 'bigger' picture of the message getting hung up on the tiny details. No disrespect.

As God ordains and anoints man, blessings flow from the head to the beard to the skirt (Psalm 133:2). Wo-man, being taken from the rib of man, is designed to be a helpmeet to man (Genesis 2:18). This is where the message gets a little sticky. But I am going to continue to give it like it was given to me. So, if I pass by you, I am not expecting you to look my way. But think about it like this. Although 'being called to the carpet' never feels good. But just know, God is never trying to take something from us. In all that we go through, God is always trying to add something to us. And this is our opportunity for growth in God. Growth in your faith in God. Growth in your trust in God. Growth in your desire to want to please God. Growth in wanting to walk uprightly. Because of the injustices that a lot of our men have been thrusted into, I believe it has left our women being put into a role that was not initially the overall scheme of things. I believe this, and more factors, have contributed to why the position of the wo-man has gotten derailed. I want you to think about how the position of wo-man has been altered. If we look back from where God has brought us from, we may not be where we want to be, but I Thank God for where He has brought us to. Women have come a long way. And we are still evolving. If we just look back, and some of us do not have to look that far back, women have blasted significantly through the roof. Whereas we were just considered to be domesticated and somewhat illiterate, we have surpassed those opinions. Look around you. Women are doing the dang thing. Women are our doctors. Women are our political officials. Women are our teachers and professors. Women are our police and firewomen. Women are our pastors. Women are our vice president. Go Kamala! Women are dominating the game. And we are proud of these strong, intelligent, and inspiring women. Not only did we conquer these roles we are pushed into, but we 'leveled up' and created some new roles.

However, I understand that in order to be a good leader, you have to learn how to be a good follower. But what happens when you are the boss at work, and you do not know how to shut it off when you get home? What happens when you are always in that 'leadership' type of role, even at home? What happens when you do not allow your husband to 'wear the pants' in the household? What happens when you do not submit to your husband? Yes. I did say the word 'submit.' By no means, am I talking about submitting to no fool though. Wives submit as your husband submit himself unto God (Ephesians 5:22). If he is submitting to God's will for the house, you should not have a problem playing your position. As your husband submits to God and tries to live righteously, you support and pray for that man. You are there to help him meet the plans that God has for your marriage. You are not there to dictate the plans. Or even create the plans. Give him the support and encouragement he needs to continue seeking wisdom from God for the marriage, for the children, for the house hold. And I promise you, God will bless you. The Bible tells us in Proverbs 18:22 that when a man finds a wife, he finds a good thing. There is a conjunction that some of us miss. A conjunction is a connecting word. It combines statements together. So, if part 'a' of the sentence is true, then part 'b' of the sentence is also true. Verse 22 goes on to say, "And, he (the husband) also receives favor with the Lord." Do you not understand what it means to have God's favor on your life? God's favor will open doors no man can shut. God's favor can open up windows from heaven and pour out blessings you do not have room enough to receive (Malachi 3:10). God's favor will cause men to give unto your bosom; pressed down, shaken together, and running over (Luke 6:38). God's favor will prepare a table before you in the presence of your enemies (Psalm 23:5). God's favor will allow your gifts to make room for you (Proverbs 18:16). God's favor will cause you to increase in the time of famine (i.e., COVID-19). God's favor will cause the womb of a barren woman to open up and give life (2 Kings 4: 11-1 7). God's favor will allow water to flow out from a rock (Psalm 78:16). God's favor will allow a valley of dry bones to be resurrected (Ezekiel 37:1-14). God's favor allows a sinner, as myself, to be covered by grace (1 Peter 4:8). God's favor is like always walking under an open heaven. Do not discredit God's favor. All the money in the world. All the degrees in the world. All the intelligence in the world cannot take the place of God's favor. God wants favor for your life. God wants favor over your household. God wants favor over your marriage. Do not take God for granted. Do not take God's favor for granted. Do not take God's grace for granted. God wants to bless you. We are God's favor demonstrators in the earth realm. Our marriages are a demonstration of God's favor in the earth realm. So, walk in it. It belongs to you.

However, this is where a lot of us get stuck. You have accomplished so much in life. You have multiple degrees. People may even call you Dr. So-In-So. People come to you for advice and resolution. You got it going on. You ain't submitting to no man. Here is where I have a problem with that. And remember, I am telling you what I know and not what I have heard. When you met that man, you knew his credentials. When you met that man, you knew his employment. When you met that man, you knew the income he was drawing in. Now since you are married, what is changed? You got your degree. You got a promotion. You got your own business. If your husband was good enough to encourage you while you were trying to get yours, what changed? What he is bringing to the table is no longer good enough? Really. When did you become Miss High and Mighty? When did you become so indignant? Here lies the beginning of the disrespect. Here lies the beginning of sowing seeds of self-pride. This is definitely a "what-nots" to do in marriage. Because, before you realize it, you are walking out of order. You are walking in disobedience to God's Word. Can I share something with you? It does not matter how many degrees you have. It does not matter how many letters you have behind your name. It does not matter how many employees come to you for guidance and problem-solving. It does not matter how many zero's you have on your paycheck. God's order will not be tainted because of your overzealous attitude.

In my book, "From Trial to Test to Testimony...

The Promise of Eden," I talk about how I went through a season of humbling. I do not believe God took me through this season because I needed it. For I trusted my husband with everything I had. What was mine, was his. And vice versa. I believe that God was taking me through that season because of where He was taking us to. And He did not want me to get there and get 'tha big head' and mess things up. Because I have been fortunate enough to be able to have acquired two degrees; one of them being my doctorate degree. So yes, we have been blessed to be able to live comfortably. But when we were going through this humbling and pruning season, my degree did not take precedence over God's order and His System. You have to read about it in the book. But just know. God lifted my husband to a place of providing for our family when I was not able to even contribute. Not one cent. Zilch. Nada. Nothing. But God ALWAYS sustained us. God was not going to let me walk in disobedience to His Word. So, ladies, be proud of your accolades. Be proud of your accomplishments. Be proud of your contributions. Kudos to you!!! Just allow God to show you how He wants to use you in the role that He has called you into.

Chapter 7

What-Nots #3

Do not be Afraid to Give Your Heart ...

Y ou have heard the saying, "Whatever you did to get him(her) is the same thing it is going to take to keep them?" I did not really appreciate this statement until I realized "I" was the one who had defaulted on it. Since I am being honest, in the beginning of my relationship with my husband, I thought I was showing him the "real" me. At least, the only "real" me that I have ever known. The "real" me that I had gotten so comfortable being. Little did I know though, I was only sharing a part of myself with my husband. It was not because I did not want to. But I realized that 1was stuck. I was stuck emotionally. I was stuck mentally. I was stuck spiritually. I was just stuck. But the irony of everything was that I was complacent in my "stuck-ness." If you have read my book, "Growing Up In Marriage ... Perfectly Flawed," you will understand why it was that I was stuck on so many different levels. I had so many unaddressed issues that never got resolved from my childhood. So, they just carried over into my adulthood. They carried over into my relationships. They carried over into my marriage. It was a hot mess! My husband would pour and pour his heart out to me and no matter how I thought I was doing the same, I was not. It was only so far; I would allow my heart to open up. I would try. But I never really succeeded at doing so on my own. And you know what else? I was even unable to talk about why I did know how to open up. I am telling you. A real hot mess! The same thoughts and unbelief that is probably going through your head right now, are the same thoughts, and more, my husband was experiencing. So, it is an understatement to say that I came off as emotionally distant, shutoff/down and unconcerned. I came off like I did not care. But that was so far from the truth.

After years of going through this unproductive cycle, there was a strain of stagnancy that began to show on the relationship. So much so, that he went one way, and I went the other.

It was during this time of my 'alone time' that I became 'woke.' 'Woke' to finally understanding the totality of everything that had just happened. Finally understanding the totality of everything that had been happening. And hopefully preventing the past from repeating itself. So, I thought. I thought. And I thought some more. The one thing I had time for was time. Time to think. Time to cry. Time to be depressed. Time to drink. Time to eat. Time to start this cycle all over again. And it was not until I got tired of being sick and tired that I decided that something had to be done. At that time, I had no idea what that was. However, I was prompted just to go and stand in front of the mirror. A mirror that would reflect me from head to foot. So, that is what I did. When I looked at myself in the mirror, I did not recognize the person staring back at me. I did not know who this person was. And the sad reality of it all was that I always considered myself to be that person to keep it 100. I did not look real at all. In my eyes, I looked like a counterfeit $100. I looked like a stranger living inside my body. There was a stranger who had been sleeping in my bed. There was a stranger who had been wearing my clothes. There was a complete stranger that was staring back at me and it frightened me. Can I be candid? It was not until this moment, when I was all completely exhausted and drained, that I cried out to God for help. Do not get me wrong, I was distraught that my marriage was in the predicament that it was in. But, if my husband wanted to reconcile today, I would be going back to the same old issues. This was an opportunity for me to work on me and how I could change my own actions. My actions which contributed to him wanting to leave the marriage. My actions which contributed to him feeling insecure as a man. My actions which contributed to him feeling unwanted. My actions which contributed to him feeling unloved. My actions were all on me. How could I demean the one person in this world that I wanted to spend the rest of my life with? How could I not give him my heart totally? How could I not love him completely? How could I 'not' so many things? What I did not realize at the time was the Iyanla Vanzant season I was about to go through.

This season for me has been a season of healing. It was during this time that I resurfaced and addressed all those little 'charms' that had been buried from years past. Those little 'charms' that had affected how I viewed life. Those little 'charms' that had affected how I viewed relationships. Those little 'charms' that affected how I even viewed myself. And to be honest, some of those little 'charms' that resurfaced, either I had forgotten about or I did not even realize how they had influenced me. One of the major little 'charms' that I dreaded having to deal with, but had to, was being molested. At a young age of maybe 7 or 8 years old, I was molested by a family member. I do not recall how long it lasted. But I can tell you this, it happened one too many times! I am forty-eight years old and I am now understanding how that trauma affected my views, actions, and responses to love. With that being my first experience with what I believed 'love' to be, my first introduction of intimacy, had been scarred. My first introduction of intimacy had been perverted. My first introduction of intimacy had been violated and taken away from me. During my marriage, I never fully under stood why I struggled in this area, until now. Because I never told anyone of what was going on, no one knew. No one could help me. And I remember meditating one day when the Holy Spirit revealed to me that what happened to me was not my fault. What happened to me I did not enjoy. Let me just say this. I said 'enjoy' because the enemy tried to convince me that because I was silent, that must have meant that I was enjoying what was happening to me. I was accepting it. Lies! I did not like it. I did not accept it. I just did not know how to handle it. I was 7 years old! I was just numb and dumb founded. What happened to me was an act of control and manipulation by my molester. I was innocent. I was the victim. And 'that' person took my innocence and purity away from me and violated it. And the only way I knew how to deal with it and protect myself was to shut down emotionally to prevent myself from being put in any situation like that ever again. That is why I always shielded away from being intimate. Because somewhere in the back of my mind, I was still trying to protect myself. And if you are wondering, no, I did not need to protect myself from my husband. I could have trusted him. I just did not know how to do that. Because I believe with everything in me that if he had known all that I had been through, we could have dealt with this together. But, since I did not give him the opportunity, I do not hold him accountable for his actions. Because remember, all this just resurfaced. So, my old tactic of self-preservation would kick in. And I would go into defense mode. Still trying to protect myself. Protect myself by guarding my heart. Protect myself by putting up a wall 'yay' high. Protect myself by not fully letting no one in. I thought I trusted people. But I realized I did not fully trust like I thought. My trust had been broken early on by someone that said they loved me. Again, somewhere in my finite mind, my ritual was that if I put my wall up, then maybe no one would be able to get that close to me and hurt me all over again. Maybe I would not get violated again. Maybe I would not get traumatized again. Maybe I would not have to feel that kind of pain again. I do not know if I was right or wrong in my actions. At the time, I did what I knew to do. And I own that. I do know this, I never meant to hurt anyone because of my actions. Especially not my husband.

As an adult, I can think of so many different ways I could have dealt with the molestation. First off, I should have told someone. But can I share something with you? Look at this from the mind of a child, okay? Molestation is a mind game. Molesters typically abuse kids that are entrusted in their care. Why? Because the child trusts them, and the child believes the molester loves them. So, why would they hurt them? If someone that says they love me, and it is someone that I trust, then why would I want to tell? Are they really abusing me? Told you. Mind games. I mean. I am sure the molester tells the child, "Everybody is doing it. Or this will make you a grown-up." All lies! But again, molestation is all about manipulation. I am going to say it over and over and over and over. Molestation is all about mind games. And once that molester has gained the trust of the 'targeted' or 'intended' child to 'be silent,' why would they stop? They have 'hit the jackpot' somewhere in their sick twisted mind. Molestation, unfortunately, happens all too often. And the molester just goes on with their life like nothing has ever happened. They keep going to work. They keep going to church. They keep showing up at family functions. They keep coming to the birthday parties. They keep coming to the graduations. They just keep on going like they are oblivious to what they have been doing to you. How is a child supposed to deal with that? How is the child supposed to respond? How is the child supposed to embrace them with hugs and kisses after having experienced them on a different 'inappropriate' level? How do you 'fake' that? All the while, the child is stuck. Stuck with questions like, "Why me? Why did this happen to me? I thought they loved me. How could they treat me like that? What did I do to them to want to 'target' me? Was I bad? Did I deserve that?" I did not know "I" had become this child screaming on the inside from my adult body. I should have yelled, "Stranger danger." The only problem was that my molester was not a stranger. And I did not realize that I was in danger. But here I was, stuck. Stuck because by no means, should a child have to carry that much of a burden around for so long. It was not their fault. It was not my fault. I should not have had to deal with the guilt and shame of being violated. I was the victim here. But again, coming from a child's mind, burying it was the best option for me. It was the only thing I knew how to do at the time. And I became a pro at burying things. Or better yet, I became a pro at 'sweeping things under the rug.' But hear me close. That pile of 'junk' under that rug will eventually start seeping from under that rug and spilling into every aspect of your life. So, my advice to you: Use your voice. Speak out. Do not keep silent. Situations cannot change if you do not make anyone aware of what is going on. Want to know why breaking your silence helps? And I am telling you what I know and not what I have heard. Because breaking your silence is the first step in quieting the mental torment that the enemy has been taunting you with. Because once you break your silence, the enemy knows you are on your way to seeing him for what he is --a liar! And, because once you break your silence, the enemy knows you are on your way to seeing God for who He is --your Redeemer. Your Savior. Your Confidant. Your Vindicator.

Your Healer. You will eventually have to trust someone. Why not start now?

Now, if the molestation was not enough, it was also during this season of healing, that I realized that there were other issues that had compounded on top of that to further make me feel unvalued as a woman. There were a couple of other circumstances that sealed this coffin for me. The first instance was when I was told, as a teen, that I would probably never be able to have children; naturally, that is. I was told that because of my hormonal imbalances I would always have to be on some type of supplemental hormonal medication. And the coup de gras, is that this medication could potentiate some unwanted side effects. Such as, they could affect my body "maturing" (i.e., puberty development, sexual urges and desires, and menstruation problems). Oh, I am not done yet. There is a little bit more. And, if this were not enough, with how I was feeling on the inside, I needed the encouragement, or the comfort, on the outside from the one person I thought could validate my existence. Validate my meaning. Validate my insecurities. Validate my vulnerabilities. Validate my worth. Validate my life. Validate my value as a woman. I needed that validation from my father. But I never got it. It is one thing to be told "You are so pretty." But it is another thing to actually feel or believe like you are worth something. Psst ... can you tell how low my self-esteem was? I did not know I needed that. I thought that by acting upset growing up would have eliminated all those feelings. I thought that by not having him around would have made it easier to stay mad at him. I thought that by not talking to him would have made me love him less. Wishful thinking. Because it did not. I needed him. Point. Blank. Period. I needed my Daddy to instill in me my worth and value. I needed my Daddy to show me how a man is supposed to treat a woman. I needed my Daddy to tell me I was beautiful even if I did not feel it. I needed my Daddy to tell me that I was complete even when every doctor told me that I was 'dysfunctional.' I needed my Daddy to tell me that life was full of possibilities. Instead of feeling like I was always inadequate or feeling empty inside. I needed my Daddy to tell me that I was worth it. I needed my Daddy to tell me that he loved me. And the irony is, I never thought I needed my Daddy for anything. But I did. He just was not there. Even though my husband put me on a pedestal. Even though my husband would tell me I was beautiful. Even though my husband would tell me all the time how much he loved me, I did not know how to receive it. I guess because a part of me did not really believe that I deserved to be loved. I mean, my own Daddy did not show me love. So, why would I expect another man to? I did not know I was scarred from that relationship, or lack thereof. Due to my own insecurities. Due to my own feelings of feeling unvalued. Due to my own feelings of feeling unworthy. Due to my own feelings of feeling unattractive. Due to my own feelings of feeling like a failure as a woman. Due to my own feelings of feeling unwanted. Due to my own feelings of feeling unloved. I gave all my highend Louis Vuitton baggage to my husband to carry. Not only was that unfair, but unbeknownst to him, he did not even know that I had given it to him to handle for me. And sadly enough, I was also clueless that I had even given him such a grave responsibility.

The "me" you see today is not the "me" from years past. Just like COVID-19 brought about a "new normal," my separation brought about a "new" me as well. If I had to hand-pick one thing that I know God has restored me from, is my silence. Did you know that life and death is in the power of your tongue (Proverbs 18:21)? That is why, I believe, the enemy fights us so hard for our voice. Because he knows if we use our voice, we will start speaking over our circumstances. If we use our voice, we will start calling those things that are not as though they are (Romans 4: 17). If we use our voice, we will speak those promises that God says belong to His children. If we use our voice, demons tremble at the name of Jesus (James 2:19). If we use our voice, we will begin to speak to those mountains trying to impede our way(Matthew 17:20). If we use our voice, we will break strong-holds and generational curses. If we use our voice, we will start speaking victory over our home. Over our children. Over our health. Over our jobs. Over our minds. Over our obstacles. Over our marriages. Over our life. That is why the enemy wants to keep you silent. Because you are a weapon when you open your mouth!

If I can impart anything into you, it is to not be afraid to open up. Do not be afraid to let people get close to you. Do not be afraid to trust your spouse with your heart. They love you and they are not there to judge you. They will not condemn you. They will not mock you. They will just love you. Love you through your pain. Love you through your agony. Love you through your trauma. Love you through your mistakes. Love you through your flaws. Love you through your setbacks. Love you even through your bad choices. If I could go back to my younger self, there are so many "what-nots" I would have addressed. So many "what-nots" about what my perception of how I thought intimacy should look. So many "what-nots" about how not everyone is out to betray your trust. Everyone's agenda is not to shatter your trust. So many "what-nots" about how I dealt with the feeling of being unwanted and broken. So many "what-nots" about not feeling or knowing how to show love appropriately. Let my story be a steppingstone for you. I say a steppingstone because I do not want you to get 'stuck' where I got stuck. Use my experiences to step higher to where God wants to take you. Where God wants to take your life. Where God wants to take your marriage. Just like God can use all that the enemy meant for bad in my life (Genesis 50:20), He is and able do the same for you. The question is," Will you be willing to stand exposed in your mirror and address your little •charms?' And no matter how difficult, stand in your truth so God can heal you?" Are you willing to admit that we are all imperfectly perfect? But I have some good news ... Have you ever heard of a Man named Jesus?

Chapter 8

What-Not# 4

Small Things DO Matter...

D o not take for granted the small things. Small things like flowers for no reason or cards when there is not a special occasion. Or sim ple things like bringing the groceries in or even doing the grocery shopping. Small things like taking the trash out or doing a load of laundry. Trust me when I say, it is these small little things that demonstrate the true matters of the heart. However, when the small little things become routine, you begin to take them for granted. You take for granted the sincerity or genuineness be hind the action. When you take for granted these small little random acts of kindness, you become blind to the preciousness of the gift that God has given to you. Keep the act of the small things pure. Keep the act of the small things kind. It is these random acts of doing small things that matter. It is these random acts of doing small things that make a difference. It is these random acts of doing small things that put a smile on your face. Do you know what a bucket list is? Simply put, a bucket list is a list of all the goals you want to achieve, dreams you want to fulfill, and life experiences you wish to experience be fore you leave this earth. A bucket list encour ages you to live life to the fullest.

At one point in time of my life, I thought it would be cool to create a bucket list. But over time, that idea just flew away like the wind. However, being in the midst of the current situ ation that I am going through, I picked back up the idea and created me a brand-new bucket list. Since I am so candid, my 'real' reason for creating a bucket list was because in my mind, I needed something to look forward to. I needed some thing to get out of bed for. I needed something to put a smile on my face. I needed something that I believed would help me feel fulfilled. I needed something to make me feel like I was 'living' and not just alive. However, this time, my bucket list was not a list of long-term dreams or goals I wanted to achieve. My bucket list was a list of my own personal expectations that I could work on daily. You see because in my mind, I needed something to look forward to. I needed something to get out of bed for. I needed something to put a smile on my face. I needed something that I thought would make me feel fulfilled. And after going through all these antics of what I "thought" I wanted on my bucket list, I realized what I wanted to achieve on a daily basis, I have had it all along. I just did not recognize it. Without God, I can do nothing. I needed to first get into alignment with God. So, the very first thing on my bucket list was re-establishing a relationship with God. Matthew 6:3 3 was my heart scripture, "But seek first God's Kingdom and His Righteousness, and all these things will be given to you as well." If I kept my focus on God and building His Kingdom, then I trust that God would give me the desires of my heart. God would give me the desires of my bucket list. My bucket list now is in my day-to-day living. My bucket list is in submitting my entire being to God, mind, body, and soul. My bucket list now is centered on how I can be a blessing to others and how I can sow good seed. My bucket list now is not even about me. But it is about how God can use me to be His beacon of light for His Glory (Matthew 5:16).

The one thing I thought I would never do was take a person for granted. But I did. I disappointed myself. I did not always show gratitude as being a wife. I did not always show gratitude as being a loving daughter. I did not always show gratitude as being an understanding sister or friend. Taking people, especially those closest to me, for granted, is never acceptable or condoned. And, just to drive the nail a little deeper. Here are a few more "what-nots." First and foremost, nobody owes you anything. What a person does for you, they do it out of the kindness of their heart. So, when you get to the point where you begin to "expect" it rather than appreciate their kindness, your well may run dry sooner than you may think. Secondly, always use your manners. As children, we were all taught manners. Now, whether we use them or not, we should have at least been taught them. So, use your words. "Please" and "Thank you" and "Your welcome," can go a long way. It is when you show appreciation that folks do not mind doing things for you. So, be courteous. Even if it is to the person you have been lying beside for years. Thirdly, marriage is about a give and take. The responsibility of the house, the responsibility of the children, the responsibility of the finances, the responsibility of everything, should not be a oneman job. True, the man is the head. But if the woman, his wife, is not his helpmeet, what is your purpose? You are there to uplift him, encourage him, be his cheerleader, support him, and love him. I believe that behind every good man is a woman. So, be "that" woman to your husband. Lastly, be mindful of who you confide in. Just because a person has ears does not mean that they should have the privilege of being your sounding board. If your confidant cannot offer you Godly wisdom, that may not be the confidant you need. Listen or do not listen. I had to learn some of these lessons the hard way. Finding 'love' is not guaranteed. So, when you do, learn to appreciate these little treasures in the people that God has given you. Value these folks because their love for you is priceless and undeserved. You cannot put a price tag on love. You cannot put a price tag on sharing memorable moments. You cannot put a price tag on the smile you give when you catch one each other's eye from across a crowded room. You cannot put a price tag on sharing a warm hug. If COVID-19 has taught us anything, it is that time is not promised. Death has no age. Race. Gender. Or socioeconomic class. So, value the time that you have today with the people who mean the most to you. For when tomorrow comes, one of you may not be there.

The Bible clearly teaches us that God is a God who blesses order (I Corinthians 14:33). God first. Husband answers to God. Wife submits to husband as he follows Christ. When you buck God's System, you are walking in disobedience and rebellion. Otherwise, if you are walking in any way contradictory to the ways of Christ, you are walking not only out of order, but you are walking in disobedience. You are walking in disorder. In 2 John 1:6, it declares, "And this is love: that we walk in obedience to God's commands and His command is that we walk in love. Walking in unappreciation in your marriage is out of order. Walking in "taking your spouse for granted" is out of order. There is predominantly one basis for why Christ gave His life for us. And that is because of love. If we are Christ-ians and profess that Christ lives in us, then our actions should be demonstrated like that of Christ in 2 Corinthians 13:4-7 (Love is patient and kind. Love is not jealous, it does not brag, and it is not proud. Love is not rude, it is not selfish, and it cannot be made angry easily. Love does not remember wrongs done against it. Love is never happy when others do wrong, but it is always happy with the truth. Love never gives up on people. It never stops trusting, never loses hope, and never quits). Every action. Every behavior. Every response should be rooted in the ways of Christ. Every response should be rooted in Christ's infinite and unblemished love. And, doing this makes you able to love humbly and unconditionally. Because you know you do not deserve it. Having the love of Christ makes you able love with gratitude. Because you know you did not do anything to earn it. Having the love of Christ makes you able to love respectfully. Having the love of Christ makes you not love begrudgingly. Having the love of Christ makes you able to love with no strings attached. Having the love of Christ makes you able to love pure. Having the love of Christ makes you able to love someone who is perfectly flawed; like me.

Chapter 9

The Pieces Will Fit...

Have you ever had like these random thoughts before you started praying? I mean like random thoughts of past choices or mistakes? Well, this particular morning, I knew I NEEDED to pray. But honestly, I did not know WHAT I was going to pray for. It was my day off and my plan was just to Netflix and chill all day. However, there was an interruption in my plan. I was prompted to immediately get up and pray. I can not say that 'prompting' ever happened before while just watching a movie. So, this was kind of like a first. So, in my obedience, I went to go and pray. But, before I began to pray, the enemy was trying to trap my thoughts and make me feel like I had nothing to be grateful for. But God. He sent me a rope. And there was this one phrase that just kept ringing in my spirit. And I remember I kept thanking God for making the pieces fit. I did not really understand what that statement really meant. But no matter how I tried to stray away from it, it just kept getting stirred in my spirit. Then God graciously showed me a vision. I was at my mother's house watching her work on one of her puzzles. And I believe this puzzle had over 1,000 pieces. So, it was a fairly large and challen ging puzzle. My mother is an avid puzzle put-to gether(er) and she prides herself on being able to complete them. Well, with this particular puzzle, she was having a problem. The problem was that there was a puzzle piece that was oddly shaped. So oddly shaped that she felt like the manufac turer made a mistake and she wanted to call them because now she was unable to complete her puzzle. And it was here that God kept saying, "I am going to make the pieces fit. I am going to make the pieces fit. No matter how oddly shaped the piece is, I am going to make the pieces fit to gether. You can even compare them against the shapes of all the other pieces. And it will still look odd. But, trust me, I am going to make the pieces fit. That one piece does not have to look like all the others. Just know. I am going to make the pieces fit. There is no need to call the manufacturer. I Am The Manufacturer. I created you. I have made provisions for you. I Am The Manufacturer over your life, and I am going to make the pieces fit. Trust Me. Do not get hung up on hurrying up and trying to rush to complete the puzzle. In due timing, I am going to make the pieces fit. The same way I told you to fore write what I knew you were going to need to get through this day; I am going to make the pieces fit. Even though the enemy tries to contaminate your thoughts with your past, I am going to make the pieces fit. Everyone wants to finish the process quickly. But I have to take you through the process so your mindset will be different after I bring you through. I have to take you through the process so your gratitude will be different after I bring you through. I have to take you through the process so your thankfulness will be different after I bring you through. I have to take you through the process so your faith will be different after I bring you through. I have to take you through the process so your heart will be different after the process. Do not rush the process. Trust Me. I am going to make the pieces fit. All that you feel like you have lost. I am going to make the pieces fit. All that you feel like was taken away. I am going to make the pieces fit. All that you feel like time has dissipated. I am going to make the pieces fit. All I need you to do is trust Me. I am going to make the pieces fit."

When the enemy tries to whisper sweet nothings in your ear. When life hits you so hard that you do not know your left from your right. When it looks like nothing is going right in your life. Your life may seem like it is in a million little pieces. Your life may seem like it is hopeless. Your life may seem like there is no way God can fix this. I am a living witness. If God can take my pieces. All my vulnerabilities. All my mistakes. All my flaws. All my insecurities. All my brokenness. All my heartache. All my shame. All my guilt. All my embarrassment. All my insufficiencies. I am crazy enough to believe that God can do the same for you. Like that puzzle my Mother wanted to return to the manufacturer because the piece looked like it did not fit, Our Manufacturer does not make mistakes. And neither are the pieces that He makes. When all is said and done, I promise you, God will make all your pieces fit. In your relationships. In your marriage. In your life.

Chapter 10

What-Nots #5

Never Say Never...

We have all heard the terms, "Side-chick," "Side-piece," or "Girlfriend with a wife on the side," right? Well, they all basically mean the same. I grew up hearing this slang more often than I care to really admit. You see, the men in my family are what you would call 'eye candy.' And women, they did not help the situation at all. They just allow these men to treat them just any old kind of way. So, it was not uncommon for both the side-piece and the wife to both show up at family bar-b-que. Never in my wildest dreams would I have thought I would end up being one of these women. At some point in the game, we have all either known or been one of these 'color ful' women. But, as I have grown older, I often ask myself, "Where is the glory in being a side-chick? Where is the honor in being a side-chick? Where is the integrity in being a side-chick? Where was the humor in my actions? Where were my morals or integrity? Why on earth did I ever think this was cute? Why did I ever think that being in this role was some sort of compli ment or something? To get my rent paid? Or to get my car note or light bill paid? To have 'blow' money? Was I that desperate?" I cannot speak for no one else. Only myself. So, for me, my choices and decisions had a lot to do with immaturity. Immaturity dealing with my emotions. Imma turity dealing with my choices. Immaturity deal ing with my feelings. Immaturity dealing with my heart. Immaturity dealing with my body.

When I was younger, much younger and very immature, I actually fooled around with a mar ried man. A married man with a whole wife and children at home. With how I was raised I knew better than to fool around with a married man. But I allowed myself to get 'caught up' in the moment. Flaunting, so to speak, that I had another woman's man. And that she must have not been doing something right at home if I was able to take her man. You know, all that "stuff" we tell ourselves to build up our ego as women. And let me tell you how the enemy baited me in and tried to convince me that what I was doing was copacetic. I ain't gonna lie to you. It was great! Considering it was hard for me to unguard my heart, this was my cup of tea. No emotional attachment was required. No feelings were needed. No expectations were defaulted on. No dating or courting was even expected. For lack of a better way to say it, I had put myself on clearance. And had marked myself down to almost being free. But, at the end of the day, no matter how great I thought it was at the time, I was still committing adultery. On the cool, I was trying to make someone else's man my man. My actions were all out of control. My actions were reckless. My actions were outside of the boundaries of being disrespectful. I violated the sanctity of another woman's marriage. I violated the commitment of another woman's marriage. I violated the covering of another woman's marnage.

From a woman's point of view, especially growing up around it, I should have been smarter about the type of seeds that I was sowing. And yes, I was still going to church this whole time. On Sundays, it was the Lord's Day. It was Monday through Saturday that was a mess! And to be quite frank, I have always had a church home. So, going to church was not a stretch for me. A lot of us go to church and still do the same things we do the rest of the week. I just did not have a relationship with God. Big difference. When you have a relationship with God, you want your choices to be different. When you have a relationship with God, you want God to order your steps. When you have a relationship with God, you want to live uprightly. When you have a relationship with God, you want to please Him. If I had had a 'real' relationship with God years ago, maybe my choices would have been different. I cannot say. But I can say this: People do what you inspect and not what you expect. I believe if my heart was postured properly towards the things of God, towards God's Will, I do not think that I would have been doing at least half of the things that I knew were wrong. All because I knew in my heart 'Who' I was trying to please.

Okay. Are you ready for this? Ready. Set. Go. Infidelity was never really an issue in our marriage; until I made it one. I really go into detail in my book, "Growing Up In Marriage ... Perfectly Flawed." But, just to recap. I committed adultery (emotionally) once in my marriage. I say emotionally because I never had any physical contact with the guy. We probably talked on the phone a few weeks or so. I do not recall the exact time length. But I am owning it. I am not proud of it. But yes. I did do that. Also, I had a 'white coat' crush on one of my doctors. If you do not know what a 'white coat' crush is, it is where you develop a crush on someone in an authoritative position. It could be your professor. A physician. A chemist. Your eye doctor. Basically, anyone who wears a white coat. So, of course, that did not go anywhere. But, in both instances, I cheated because I allowed my attention to be distracted from where it should have been. I allowed my conversation to get sparked from where it should have been. I was wrong. At the time, I did not really know how to explain my actions. Because honestly, I did not know where they were coming from. I just kind of kept silent and acted like it should not have been that big of a deal. Remember when I said I was immature? Do you see it yet? Anyway, there were several times when I should have reassured my husband that his "perception" of what he thought was going on was only that, perception. But I did not. I just kind of swept his feelings under the rug. Thinking things would just blow over and we could forget about it. How many of you know that NEVER works? Do I really need to tell you "what-nots" to do? I think I have done a pretty good job of making it clear for you. But, if you still need a "what-nots," how about these two: 1) TAKE YOURSELF OFF CLEARANCE. God has given me grace to be able to share my experiences with you. Do not take God's grace for granted. Do not take your spouse's grace for granted. The one thing you never want to do is be looking for water, thirsty, and the well is dry. And 2) Girl, BE BETTER THAN

ME. And the only way I was able to do that was with The Word of God. When God began to show me, and I started to believe, who He said I was in Him, everything began to change. My vow to God and my desire to have a relationship changed. My vow to my marriage and what it should have been all along began to change. I could not truly honor my husband if I did not honor God first. I could not uplift my husband if I did not know how to give God glory. I could not love my husband ifl have never truly understood, or even received, the sacrifice oflove that Christ had displayed for me. So, I had to align some things differently in my life. My thinking had to be restored in the Word of God. My heart had to be purified in the Word of God. My body had to be sanctified in the Word of God. Honey, you are gonna need God to get you through this. But good news, they (you & me) overcame by the word of their testimony (Revelations 12:11). Can you do me this one favor though? When you get stronger, can you reach back and help pull up someone else (Luke 22:32)? Gracias.

Chapter 11

What-Nots #6

Tick...Tick...Boom...

I can remember when I was back in pharmacy school some umpteen years ago. This was prob ably the first time I REALLY ever had to study. Not being cocky or anything, but I was always able to kind of "pick up" on lessons from my schoolwork. And even though I already had my bachelor's degree in Biology when I entered pharmacy school, this level of coursework caught me off-guard. It was a booger. I remember I used to have to take these caffeine tablets, called Vivarin, to help me stay awake because it did not seem like I had enough hours in the day to get done what I expected to accomplish. No matter how much time I put into my lesson, I never seemed to have enough time. Not enough time to study. Not enough time to go to the lab. Not enough time to go over my notes. Not enough time to make corrections. I just seemed to never have enough time. I felt like I was drowning. But even though I felt like I did not have enough time, I STILL put all I had into making the most of my time. Have you ever heard the saying,"You put time into what you want to put time into?" Well, that statement is all the way true. Think about it. If something interests you, that "some thing" has your undivided attention. You are willing to devote every single iota of your time. You will stay up all night for that "something." Or you may even get up 3 hours early just to give "that" something the attention you want to give it. On the flipside, if you have zero level of inter est, guess what? You could care less if that "something" gets done or not. Well, the same ap plied to my situation. I wanted my degree. I wanted my Doctorate. I wanted to succeed. I wanted to pass my classes. I wanted to graduate. And I wanted to succeed in life. So, I put all my effort into making sure I accomplished these goals. And with the grace of God, those goals came to pass. I put in the work. I devoted my time. Time that was precious. Time that could not be replaced. Time that was not taken for granted. Time that proved to be beneficial. What a go getter? Right? Maybe. But why did I not have that same tenacity when it came to my marriage? Why did I not put in the "time" into making sure my marriage grew and sustained? Why did I not pull all-nighters like I knew how to do from being in college? Why did I not take Vivarin to make sure I stayed "woke" during the most critical hours of my marriage? I could ask the "why" question over and over and over again until I was blue in the face. If I was a go-getter in every other aspect of my life, why was I not a gogetter in my marriage? You may not be ready for my answer. But the only way I am trying to learn how to live is by being honest. So, here it goes. I took my husband, his kindness and his efforts for granted. I could buy my husband a brandnew Phantom Rolls Royce. But all that did not matter because all he wanted was my time. Time to get to know me. Time to be intimate with me. Time to make more memories with me. Time to simply love me and get inside my heart. I had never met anyone that wanted to get to know "me" on that level. So, that was all new for me. And honestly because I did not know how to respond, most times, I did not. I know I probably looked like a deer caught in headlights because I would be almost speechless. I had learned from early on that young ladies are seen and not heard. I just took that saying a little too far because I would almost be like church mouse quiet. And because I lacked in the 'verbal' department, I would try and overcompensate in other areas. And most times, it was in the area of me trying to supplement my love by giving him expensive gifts.

The reason why I reference my other book, "Growing Up In Marriage ... Perfectly Flawed" so often, is because this was my 'big reveal' book. A 'big reveal' because I had to lay to rest the old me to make room for the new me. Although this was my second book, this was my very first book about my own personal mistakes. This was my very first book about my own shortcomings. This was my very first book about my brokenness. This was my very first book about my molestation. This was my very first book about my insecurities and vulnerabilities. This was my very first book discussing all of my childhood trauma and how everything helped to shape the woman I once was. And yes, I am correct in saying 'was' because this was also my book of healing. This book has very intimate details of my exposure. Exposure which led to me being transparent. And in my transparency, I was able to stand in and own my truth. And it was here, where I got my healing. I am trying to provide you with some context so you can better understand why it was I had a wall around my heart. I am trying to get you to understand where and how action-reaction became a part of me. I am trying to get you to understand how and where at what point my actions became my defense mechanism. Trust me when I say, I am not giving you any excuses. Hello? I have been nothing but candid so far. And I do not plan on being anything but that. I just want you to be able to follow along, if you can, with how my thought processes developed.

Have you ever just wanted a do-over? Like, if you had the opportunity, you would do-over a decision you made in the past that you wish you could change now? I would not mind a doover. But, if I am being honest, I would have a few stipulations. Since this is all hypothetical, just humor me and let me tell you what I would want. I would like to have the wisdom I have now. But I would like to go back and do-over my adolescent years. Those seem to be the years that drastically changed my life. I want a Marty McFly moment like in Back to the Future. Right off the back, I would have the best, most available, most supportive, most encouraging, and most loving Daddy in the whole entire world. And I know I would just eradicate that whole molestation foolishness. Or, if I could not stop these things from happening, I would definitely have more wisdom to know how to constructively handle these 'mountains.' I definitely would not have kept silent. I definitely would not have let these do-overs emotionally, mentally, and physically torment me. I definitely would not have let these do-overs devalue my worth as a woman. I definitely would not have let these do-overs control and manipulate my responses. I definitely would not have let these do-overs keep me in bondage. You want to hear something crazy? I was able to forgive my molester quicker than I was able to forgive myself. It was hard to forgive myself because I never stood up for myself. I never spoke up. I never stopped it. Although I knew it was not my fault, those mind games the enemy tormented me with was strong. Talk about tormented thoughts. When I tell you that strong hold was immense, it was the 'real' deal. Until. And there is always an until when it comes to God. Trust me when I tell you that God will take everything that the enemy intended for bad and turn it around for good (Genesis 50:20). I cannot stress this enough. I am living it!

If the "now" me could scream back to the "then" me, I would say, "Wake up girl. The enemy is trying to destroy you and he is not going to play fair. He is going to try to use your hidden insecurities against you. He is going to try to use your molestation against you. He is going to try to use your feelings of "invalidation" with your father against you. He is going to try and make you feel like you are unworthy to be loved. He is going to try to use your feelings of never being good enough to destroy your dreams and aspirations. But if you could just see the enemy for the coward he truly and DON'T FALL FOR THE OKIE DOKE. God will use every single one of your shortcomings. God will use every single one of your mistakes. God will use every single one of your flaws for His glory. No matter what the tricks and schemes the enemy tries to use against you, he cannot win. He is under your feet (Romans 16:20)! Not all your days will be roses and daffodils. But know that even though these weapons form against you, hold firm to God's Word because they will NOT overtake you (Isaiah 54:17). You are going to have to break your silence and learn how to use your voice. Learn how to call those things that are not as though they are (Romans 4:17). Learn how to speak life over those valleys of dry bones in your life (Ezekiel 37:1-14). Learn how to use your anointing to destroy yokes (Isaiah 10:27). Learn how to use your faith-filled words to move mountains (Mark 11:23). You cannot be too shy to speak up. You cannot be too shy to stand up for what you believe is right. You are going to have to learn how to use your voice Tena. Your whole life depends on you learning to use your voice. Take the time now and learn how to use your voice to bless your future."

Now, as I have said, I did not always have a voice. Actually, I have been silent for longer than I have been talking. And for years, I lived through the torment. For years, I tried to forget about the torment. For years, I tried to 'sweep the torment under the rug.' For years, I tried to keep living like what had happened did not affect me. For years, I tried to act like my life had been 'normal.' And this charade lasted for a long time. And then the inevitable started to 'show up.' The side effects from those events that I tried to keep quiet slowly started to creep out. And you know what? Over time, I unknowingly turned from the victim into a victimizer. Hold up. Wait. Pump your brakes. Capture your thoughts. Allow me to clarify. I did NOT turn into an actual molester. But I turned into the effects from being the victim. Thereby, inflicting the same type of pain that I experienced from my trauma, onto someone else, my husband. I did not realize at the time what I was doing. Still, no excuse. But now, I am confidently able to say that it is true that hurt people do indeed hurt people. I inflicted those same feelings that I had come to know all too well of how it felt to be mistreated, neglected, and rejected. Yes, I did that. I became a victimizer. As a child, when I felt unvalued, while in my marriage, I made my husband feel unvalued. As a child when I felt unattractive, while in my marriage, I made my husband feel unattractive. As a child when I felt neglected, while in my marriage, I made my husband feel neglected. As a child when I felt overlooked, while in my marriage, I made my husband feel overlooked. As a child when I felt unloved, while in my marriage, I made my husband feel unloved. I want to be able to click my heels three times and 'blink' my way into a do-over.

So, my first little "what-nots" is to use your voice. Your voice is your weapon. Your voice is your strength. Your voice can speak life (Proverbs 18:21). Your voice is your praise. Your voice is mandated by God. Here are just a few scriptures to back me up: 1) Let everything that has breath praise the Lord (Psalm 150:6). 2) Enter His gates with thanksgiving and His courts with praise; give thanks to Him and praise His name (Psalm 100:4). 3) Lord, you are my God; I will exalt you and praise your name, for in perfect faithfulness you have done wonderful things, things planned long ago (Isaiah 25: 1). 4) Great is the Lord, and greatly to be praised. His greatness is unsearchable (Psalm 145:3). 5)

And one more from Psalm 71:8, "My mouth is filled with Your praise, and with glory all day." I chose scriptures with the word 'praise' in it because praise is an 'act' of expressing admiration. And 'act' is simply defined as when you 'do' something. Praising will require you actually doing or using something. And that something is your voice.

As you use your voice, the enemy gets nervous. Using your voice will not stop bad things from happening to you. But what you speak will surely determine how you respond to it. From the abundance of the heart, the mouth speaks (Matthew 12:34). Using your voice will expose the enemy when he comes up against you. Using your voice will bring those things that happen in the dark into the light. Using your voice will show the enemy that you are not afraid of him because God does not give us the spirit of fear. But, of power, love, and a sound mind (2 Timothy 1:7). Here is another little "what-nots" for you, stop allowing the enemy to keep your mind in agony. True. You have had a hard childhood. True. You have made some choices that you wish you could take back. True. You may have some regret about some things that may have happened over the years. But here is a reality check. Can you change the past? No, you cannot. Pick yourself up. Repent. Learn from your mistakes. And walk by faith one faith step at a time. Once you have repented, then you are forgiven. God is not holding anything against you. God has actually forgotten about it (Hebrews 8:12). That is not God trying to make you feel guilty. That is the enemy that keeps bringing up your mistakes. It is the enemy that constantly reminds you of the 'bad' person God thinks you are. It is the enemy that taunts you day in and day out. I know this torment. Trust me. I lived with it for a long time. No, I am not proud of how I allowed my circumstances to 'show up' in my marriage. No, I am not proud that I am separated from my husband when I thought we would grow old together. No, I am not proud of a lot of things. But I had to do what I am telling you to do. "Whatnots" to do just to keep your sanity. "What-nots" to do just to keep a smile on your face. "Whatnots" to do just to be able to get up out of the bed in the morning. "What-nots" to do just to have some peace in my life. Bottom line: Stop giving the enemy access to torment you. When the enemy comes at you, throw this back at him, "We take captive every thought to make it obedient to Christ (2 Corinthians

10:5)" and tell him to get that mess out of here! See, once you know The Word, that IS your weapon. And you will not settle for those 'sweet nothings' that the enemy tries to whisper in your ear. If you read it in God's Word, then your response should be, "Yes God, I receive. And Amen because I am coming into agreement with what You (God) said that I can have (2 Corinthians 1:20)." Accepting anything less than that would be uncivilized. Girl, close that drive-thru!

Do not get intimidated by the enemy because the one thing he does not want you to find out about yourself is who you really are. Because once you find out who you really are in Christ, then you will find out who he really is not. He does not call the shots over your life. He does not dictate how your life is going to turn out. He may want it to look like he controls everything, but he does not. That is why he is so adamant about keeping you in the dark. That is why he is so adamant about keeping you silent. That is why he is so adamant about making you feel ashamed, embarrassed, or even guilty. That is why he fights you so hard. He does not want you to know that you are 'You.'

Do not be one of those people, like me, who thinks that you can handle everything. Do not be one of those people to hold everything in and not talk about it. Because before you know it, tick ... tick ... boom, right in front of you. And trust me, there will be casualties. So, do not ever be too proud to ask for help. Do not ever be too embarrassed to ask for help. Do not be too prideful to ask for help. Do not be too ashamed to ask for help. It is okay to ask for help sometime. God did not put us here together to live independently of each other. We need one another; whether you realize it or not. As God's children, we are many parts connected to one body---The Body of Christ. But, as long as you think 'you can handle things,' the enemy will eat your lunch right in front of you every single day. Until. There is that 'until' again. Until you get sick and tired of being sick and tired, then you will fight back. Fight back because God's Word says, "I am the head and not the tail (Deuteronomy 28:13)." Fight back because God's Word says, "Behold, I have given you authority to tread on serpents and scorpions, and over all the power of the enemy, and nothing shall hurt you (Luke 10:19)." Fight back because God's Word says, "Greater is He that is in me than he that is in the world (1 John 4:4)." Fight back because

God's Word says, "No weapon formed against me shall prosper (Isaiah 54: 17)." Fight back because God's Word says, "We are more than conquerors through Him (Romans 8:3 7)." Fight back because God's Word says, 11 But the Lord is faithful, and He will strengthen you and protect you from the evil one (2 Thessalonians 3:3)." Fight back because God's Word says, "For the weapons of our warfare are not of the flesh but have divine power to destroy strongholds (2 Corinthians 10:4)."

The enemy fights tirelessly trying to 'redefine' your identity. So, if you need a "whatnots" to do: Do not let him! Fight him with The Word. Your circumstances do not define you. Your mistakes do not define you. Your sin does not even define you. Christ took our circumstances. Our mistakes. And every single one of sins to the cross. If God casts our sins as far as the east is from the west (Psalm 103: 12), why let the enemy keep you in guilt, agony, and torment behind them?

At some point in time, you are going to have to learn how to 'fight' for you. And you are never too young, or too old, to start fighting. I wish I knew I could fight for that shattered little girl years ago. I wish I knew I could stand up for her years ago. I wish I knew a lot of things. But you have heard me say before, "It is never too late to teach an old dog new tricks." Well, guess what? This old dog is 'woke' now. This old dog is ready to fight for God's People (i.e., my family). This old dog is no longer silent. This old dog has learned a few tricks along the way. This old dog is no longer settling for what the enemy says I can have. This old dog is ready to take all that God says belongs to me. And the first thing I am taking back is my voice!

Chapter 12

What-Nots #7

Brick House 36-24-36...

Do you remember the feeling you get when you first saw your spouse? Did your stomach do cartwheels? Did your heart start fluttering? Did your palms get sweaty? Did your mouth get dry as cotton? Now, let me ask you. When you see your spouse now, do you still get any of these same feelings? If you do not, why not? What changed? Are they not the same person you fell in love with? Or have you just gotten so accus tomed to 'seeing' them on a daily basis that the small detail sometimes gets overlooked. Small details like complimenting them on their hair. Small details like telling them they smell good. Small details like noticing that they have done something different with their hair. Or even small details like telling them how handsome, or beautiful, they look today. Before I begin this, let me start by saying that my husband is one of the most handsomest men I have ever met. He is al ways well-dressed and well-groomed. And he al ways smelled good. And I am guilty because I did not tell him enough. While separated, it became easy for me to recognize things I could have done differently in my life. In my relationships. In my marriage. For starters, in my marriage, there were quite a few "what-nots" in this area. But I am going to start with allowing the spirit of complacency to dwell in me. Because I always saw my husband in his natural attractive form, I just got used to seeing him that way. I became really lazy in my compliments. I became really lazy in reminding him how I only had eyes for him. I became lazy in reassuring him that I thought he was the most attractive man I had ever seen. And how lucky I was that he had chosen me. The times my husband needed my outward attention, or affection, I was lazy. Or the times my husband needed me to stroke his ego as a man or the times my husband needed me to value his manhood, I was lazy. You should not have to "fish" for a response from your wife to help build up your husband's self-esteem. You should not have to do certain things to your body just for a response from your wife to make her feel more sexual towards you. You should not have to "search" for responses to anything "new" your husband tries. And, you know what the sad reality is? For the most part, a lot of men are much less superficial than women. And before I get some raised eyebrows, let me explain what I mean. All women are beautiful. And some of us put a lot into our looks. We go the extra extra extra mile. We pride ourselves on looking beautiful making sure our hair is on point. Making sure our faces are beat. Making sure our nails look like we could be hand models. Making sure we smell like the newest scent of the perfume out of the market. Oh, and let us not mention our attire. We are Fashion Nova'd out from head to toe. Not saying that men do not take this much grooming time because some of them do. But women, we slay. And we slay all day every day. But all this "slaying" does not keep or maintain a marriage. This next statement is a little excruciating saying out loud because I am a little embarrassed admitting. But my husband and I were that "slay" couple. We always dressed well. We were always groomed well. We always drove well. And we always lived well. However, from the inside looking out, there was so much I could have "slayed" better at There was so much that I missed. Not purposely. Just ignorantly missed. Even though I was physically present in marriage, I emotionally missed so much. So much emotionally I took for granted. So much emotionally I overlooked.

So, another "what-nots" is to just be and stay present. Be and stay present for yourself. Be and stay present for your husband. Be and stay present in your relationships. Be and stay present in your marriage. Time can evolve people. Time can evolve situations. Time can evolve circumstances. Time can evolve your entire life. I remember when my husband and I first separated, I remember apologizing to him for simply "missing" out. There were so many events. So many holidays. So many moments of intimacy. So many moments of affection. So many moments of just quality time. There were just so many occasions that I just plainly "missed." Although I apologized, I just did not understand the magnitude of what "missed" actually meant. I just did not grasp the magnitude of what it was going to take to heal through those things that I had "missed" in my marriage. I had no idea how intensely I would have to endure "mirror experiences" of what and why I had missed out on so much. I had to take ownership of why I missed the efforts of my husband's 'little' gestures. I missed the opportunities of stroking my man's ego, making him feel like his attention was the only attention I needed. I missed the small opportunities of playful foreplay. I missed the small opportunities of enjoying those quality moments of being intimate. I missed the opportunities of sharing myself completely, mind, body, and soul, with my husband. However, to understand, or even appreciate and own, and most importantly learn from these "missed" opportunities, I had to get to the root of the issue. Going back a few statements back, I said I had to have a "mirror experience." If you have read any of my other books, I talk quite a bit about these "mirror experiences." For me, this is when I stand in front of God's mirror. Being completely exposed, naked (not literally) and transparent. This is my act of presenting myself before God in my purest form. Here, I am not putting on any airs. Here, I do not have to impress God by talking prolifically or intellectually. Here, I do not have to impress God by dressing like I am just coming off the runway. Here, I do not even have to comb my hair or brush my teeth. In my "mirror experience," as I come before God, I am coming humbly. I am coming seeking restoration. I am coming seeking healing. It is in these "mirror experiences" that God shows me, ME. No matter how pretty. No matter how unpretty. It is here in God's mirror that I am reminded that I am forgiven. It is here in God's mirror that I am reminded that I am restored. It is here in God's mirror that I am reminded that by the stripes of Jesus, I am healed (Isaiah 53:5). It is here in God's mirror that I am reminded that I am loved. It is here in God's mirror that I am reminded that I am God's Masterpiece (Ephesians 2: 10). It is here in God's mirror that for all my ashes, that for all my misfortunes, that for my valley of dry bones, God gives me His beauty (Isaiah 61:3).

Have you ever heard in The Bible how you should be quick to listen and slow to speak (James 1:19)? Well, this, unfortunately, was not one of my highest attributes. This is not an excuse. This is just an explanation. By no means, am I proclaiming that my actions or reactions were right. So, the next "what-nots" is to check your attitude at the door. You are not who you think you are. Step down off your high horse and take this dose of humility. The one thing I want to stress is that you are never too old to change. You are never too old to want to be better. You are never too old to want to see a difference. You are never too old to want to be a better version of you. But here is my story. Growing up, I saw a lot of 'impatient' people. The standard I saw was that if you did not get out of the way, then you got run over. So, in my mind, I never wanted to become that type of person. How many of you can guess that I became that very person I had purposely set out not to be? I had become that 'impatient' people. The kind of 'impatient' people that I did not know I even was. The kind of 'impatient' people I never thought I could become. The kind of 'impatient' people who thought that listening quickly was more important than listening effectively and intuitively. Being in a rush can cause you to miss the 'tiny' detail. The 'tiny' detail of your husband scratching his head if he was extremely sleepy. Or the 'tiny' detail of seeing your husband roll his fingers on his belly as he talks. Or even the 'tiny' detail of watching your husband blow his hot food while it is in his mouth. You may not appreciate those 'tiny' memories then, but when you do not have them anymore, it feels like you have lost a treasure. A treasure that you now realize was priceless. A treasure that you now realize was memorable. A treasure that you now realize had so much value. Looking back in retrospect, my actions of being that kind of 'impatient' people could have easily been perceived as being curt. Curt because I was putting a time limit on my ear. When I should have seen it as a blessing that I was being trusted enough to confide in. Curt because I was forward thinking a conversation because it was not "moving along" as fast as I would have liked it to move. Curt because I was not giving my full attention to the person trusting me with their innermost thoughts and feelings. When did I become so pompous? Oh, what a tangled web I have weaved for myself.

The more and more I thought about it, falling into this 'rushed' behavior was easy for me. Everything and everyone around me was always "moving and shaking." Work, family, school, church, laundry, cleaning. Then, the cycle keeps repeating itself. Life can be so rushed. But really, what is the big rush? What are we rushing towards? What is not going to be there by the time we get there? Absolutely nothing. However, it was not until I met my husband that I saw something different. He was so laid back. He was hardly ever in a rush to do anything. It was like he enjoyed the process of things more than reaching the actual destination. I wish I had taken more time to appreciate some of the road trips rather than reaching the actual destination. So, hopefully, this next little "what-nots" will be blatantly obvious. Differences are not presented to be overlooked or disregarded. Differences are there to be appreciated, embraced, and welcomed. Differences are presented to promote patience along the journey can be enjoyed. Patience to enjoy the process. Patience to embrace the process. Patience to enjoy the memories along the way. Have you ever heard of a pearl farmer? Pearl farmers are just as the name implies. Pearl farming is the industry responsible for grafting pearl mollusks and producing cultured pearls. If you are a pearl farmer, you must have immense patience. Patience, in this instance, is needed because it can take months to years for a single pearl inside an oyster shell to develop to the desired size. Some oysters can produce two to three pearls over the course of their lifetime, but only an oyster with pearls of good quality will repeat the process of producing a pearl.

If we are lucky, we find that one special person to share our "pearl" moments with. Think about it this way. We are the pearls and God is our 'Ultimate Pearl Farmer.' Each one of us have unique talents and gifts given specifically to us by God. However, some of these "treasures" can take months or even years to cultivate to its highest level of beauty. The same way a Pearl Farmer is patient with the oyster and the pearl forming on the inside of it, is the same way God is patient with us. We do not automatically become those "pearls" that God created us to be. It takes time. We have our incubation times, or waiting room times, just like a natural pearl. The same way God was patient with us in forming the "pearls" inside of us is the same way we need to be patient with our spouses. They have "pearls" on the inside of them as well. A lot of us have read 1 Corinthians 13:4, "Love is patient, love is kind. It does not envy, it does not boast, it is not proud." I like the way The Message Bible gives a little more detail, "Love never gives up. Love cares more for others than for self. Love does not want what it does not have. Love does not strut, Does not have a swelled head, Does not force itself on others. It is not always about 'me first.'" My lightbulb moment: earlier when I commented about becoming 'pompous' or arrogant, here is where I got quickened. I was in error whenever I was strutting, pretentious, or 'lightly' persuading my views on others. All because I was thinking faster than they were talking. How disrespectful is that? That was me. I never thought that by being "rush persistent" came off as me acting like a 48-year-old toddler throwing a "me first" tantrum.

As a result of my separation, my patience is developing more and more. A friend of mine pointed out to me that my 'anxiousness' or lack of wanting to wait (i.e., impatient) was all because I did not have control. I never really saw it as that, but I understood the message. The point she was wanting me to get was that in my anxiousness and in my lack of wanting to wait, I was not giving God any room to move. Instead of making God bigger than my problem, in my anxiousness, I was allowing my problem to become bigger than my God. I was not doing this intentionally. But I took her words into consideration. And honestly, I did not even realize I was removing God's hand from over my situation. From over my life. Instead of grabbing onto God's hand, I was steadily trying to hold onto the hands of my anxiousness. I had to make a decision. I had to make a declaration. I declared that I was no longer willing to hold onto the worthless feelings of anxiousness and impatience any further. I declared that I was no longer going to be a slave to impatience or anxiousness. I declared I was released from these strongholds in Jesus' name. Life is too short and the time to embrace it is even shorter. Take the time to love. Take the time to create new memories. Take the time to have enough patience to enjoy your journey with the one God has destined to rideit out with you. Carpe Diem!

Chapter 13

What Nots #8

You're Not Always Seeing What Your Eyes Are Showing You...

I t is one thing to be accused and you actually did what you were accused of. But it is another thing to be accused and you did not do what 'they' said you did. I have been on both sides of this situation. I have been the one accusing AND I have been the one being accused. And, neither one of these 'hot' seats feel good. Here is an example of a woman who I believe we all can at least relate to. Her story is found in John 8:1-11. But to paraphrase, The Bible says that this woman was actually 'caught' in the act of adultery. She had actually done what she was being accused of. According to 'they,' she was guilty. So, she should endure the punishment, right? It amazes me how 'they' are always so quick to point the finger at someone else who has fallen and may need some grace. 'They' are always so quick to point out someone else's faults or shortcomings. 'They' are always so quick to play judge, jury, and bailiff. It sometimes baffles me how people who have received grace act like they do not remember when they got grace. They can be so indignant and forgetful at times. How ever, Matthew 7:3-5 puts this so plainly, "How are you going to point out the speck of sawdust in someone else's eye when you have a whole plank in yours?" The only difference between 'they' and the woman who was caught, is that she got caught and 'they' did not. Therefore, if your name is 'They,' then your something called "Grace" should be your best friend. But getting back to our regularly scheduled program.

When this woman, who has been identified by her sin and not even her name, was brought to Jesus, 'they' wanted to automatically condemn her of her wrongdoing. P.S. Do not let 'they' define you by your mistakes. Do not let 'they' define you by your decisions. Do not let 'they' define you by your sin. Do not let 'they' keep you oppressed by their expectations. Alright. I am done. I am stepping off my soap box now. But, back to my original point. When 'they' were trying to test Jesus to see if He would contradict the law, His response was so suave. Jesus' silence spoke volumes. He dropped the mic on 'they.' At one point, 'they' thought Jesus was ignoring them. But Jesus just bent down and began to write on the ground. Now what He wrote, I would love to know. But I do know this. Whatever it was that Jesus did write, it was enough to make 'they' silent. So silent that 'they' were no longer her accusers. So silent that 'they' no longer wanted to condemn her. So silent that 'they' were themselves convicted. So silent that 'they' remembered that time when 'they' received grace, and 'they' quietly walked away. What was so mind-blowing for me when reading this was the grace she received AND she was guilty. She had committed the crime, but she did not do any time. This woman was saved by grace. If God can give you grace when you know you are guilty, why would we not think that He would vindicate us when we are innocent?

I had put myself in a similar position, unknowingly, in my own marriage. Hopefully, you will understand what I am talking about after explaining. By the time I met my husband, I was by no means an expert at dating. I had only seriously dated maybe one guy before him. I had a few male friends. But that was it, just friends. So yes, it is true that men and women can be just platonic friends. Because I had them. However, because of my lack of maturity and insensitivity to my husband's feelings, I did not take his concerns in this area too seriously. Because I knew that I was being honest with my husband, I just assumed that he should have known that I was being honest. I had never done anything to betray his trust. So, why would there be an issue in this area? But, because I was inexperienced, immature, and insensitive, my demeanor was perceived as if I were disregarding his feelings. I had no idea that my silence was allowing a picture to be painted. A picture of deceptive perception. I never would have never put these two and two together. But since that was the 'perception,' I made little effort to correct it. This was by far, not the best way to handle things. So, you can only imagine how 'secretly' toxic this issue became over time.

But, going back to my inexperience, this did nothing but put a spotlight on my immaturity. I was immature in not recognizing the importance of security in a relationship. Security in a marriage. I was immature in not recognizing the importance of reassurance in a relationship. Reassurance in a marriage. I was immature in not recognizing the importance of nurturing in a relationship. Nurturing in a marriage. It was not until later that I realized how damaging the spirit of 'perception' can really be. Because for years, I allowed 'perception' to speak for me. For years, I allowed 'perception' to be my voice. For years, I allowed 'perception' to vindicate me. But why? Not a smart decision on my behalf, I know. Because everything that was 'perceived' was the total opposite of things that actually were. But I never spoke up. I never even tried to defend myself. I had allowed 'perception' to paint a nasty little picture of untruth. I had allowed 'perception' to paint a nasty little picture of disrespect. I had allowed 'perception' to paint a nasty little picture of bitterness. Allow me to give you a demonstration. I was thinking about a conversation that my husband and I once had. And the one thing that kept ringing in my head was my husband's concern about him feeling like he had been disrespected. This was a shock to me because I had no idea, he had even felt like this. However, I just continued to listen to him in total awe. Now, I am guilty of doing a lot of things, but this one, I never would have picked this one. From Day One, whatever I had, he had. And vice versa. Whatever we did not have, then WE did not have it. In my mind, I thought I had opened up and gave him access to every aspect of my life. So, how could he have possibly felt like "I", of all people, had disrespected him? I did not realize how much this had bothered me because this was still weighing on me from an earlier conversation. I will take ownership for a lot of things, but this one, should not have been my charge. But I listened to my husband, hearing the pain in his voice. And it broke my heart. First off because he was hurting. And secondly because he felt like I was the cause of his pain. So no, it was not the time to try and defend myself. No, it was not the time to try to explain. And no, it was not the time to try and convince him that that was never my intention. It was time to listen. And listen empathetically and with compassion. These were his feelings and the one thing I wanted to do was embrace the trust that he was giving me to share them with me. Whether you realize it or not, when someone shares their feelings with you, they are sharing a part of themselves. A part of themself that maybe you did not know about. A part of themself that is sacred to them. A part of themself that is so enduring and personal. A part of themself that may even be uncomfortable discussing. So, when listening, do just that --be quiet and listen. His feelings were real to him. His feelings were legitimate to him. His feelings were right to him. His feelings were truth to him. And 'that' is the point where it is sometimes hard to come back from. Trying to change the 'perception' of what someone believes their reality, or truth, to be. Ding. Ding. Ding. Is the "what-nots" obvious? Perception. Use your voice. Perception. Use your voice. They go hand-in-hand. I had to learn the hard way that Perception rarely says what you are actually meaning. No one can speak your thoughts like you. No one can do you, like you. No one can be you, like you. So, be you. If I have not learned anything else during this separation, it was to use my voice. The only way I could use my voice was if I silenced 'Perception.'

P.S. And when you feel weak, know that God's strength is made perfect in you (2 Corinthians 12:9).

Perception can be tricky. Because sometimes, perception can make you believe something that is not even there. And I mean you believe so hard, that your truth is formed. And no one or nothing can change your mind. Truth based from perception will never yield a fruitful harvest. Perception gets planted based off of a seed. And once that seed gets planted, it does not take much to make it grow. The same way natural plants which require water to grow and flourish, so does a spiritual seed. A spiritual seed is grown by thoughts. Thoughts that continually feed and water it. Most times, these thoughts are accusing in nature. Or it can be a condemning thought. A judgmental thought. A lying thought. A thought that gets planted by the enemy. The Bible tells us that he is the accuser of the brethren (Revelation 12: 10). And believe it, he is!

I had allowed this spirit of 'perception' to hover over my life for years now. Allowing seed after seed to get planted. A seed of 'perception' that has now grown to a real-size forest. A seed of 'perception' that has entangled in it so many different types of weeds. A seed of 'perception' that has twisted up so many truths. A seed of 'perception' that started from just a little doubt. A seed of 'perception' that was 'swept under the rug.' A seed of 'perception' that was not pulled up by its roots. A seed of 'perception' that has confused all efforts. A seed of 'perception' that has not just made holes in the bridge but may have also damaged the bridge past a point of repair. Here just a few suggestions of "What-Nots"; if you could not already guess. Do not take time or situations for granted. Do not take each other's feelings or concerns for granted. When you love someone, if they are hurting, then you are hurting. Take these times of intimate conversations seriously. Do not belittle that sensitive area of trust. Do not take those, what you may think are "irrelevant" or "silly" conversations for granted. Do yourself a favor and use your words. Use your voice. Do not let your actions always speak for you. Do not leave room for 'perception' to creep its nasty little head in your relationship. Its influence is underestimated. Also, do not take your spouse's silence for acceptance. Because someone has been holding a loaded gun for a while now, you do not want it to go off at an inopportune time. There is power in conversation. Do take your spouse's love for granted. Love is a gift. So, do not sabotage it or take it for granted.

As I was meditating on some things one day, God began speaking to me about this one specific thing --that strong spirit of 'perception' and how it had gotten rooted deep down in my spirit. And what God told me next, frightened me. Yet, it also humbled me. God told me that I was on the enemy's 'hit list.' Hit list, in the sense, that I became a centralized target when I opened my mouth and made a simple confession, as a child, to make me a humble servant unto others. Who would have thought that such a simple prayer would invite such spiritual warfare? Being innocent and excited to honor God, it was around that age that I was learning how to use my voice.

It was around that age that I was learning how to confess with my heart. It was around that age that I had made up in my mind that I was going to be 'different' because I wanted to follow Christ. However, it was not soon after that, looking back now, when 'life's struggles' began to get thrown at me. It was not soon after that, that I remember the molestation began. It was not soon after that, that my personality began to change and my insecurities from the inside were becoming evident on the outside. It was not soon after that, that my heart was broken from mistrust and I noticed I was not as 'trusting' with people with it. It was not soon after that, that my heart became saddened and unhappy. It was not soon after that when I noticed how reserved and silent, I was becoming. The list could go on and on. But I was now understanding something that was a little bit frightening. Frightening because I never considered myself to be threatening. Threatening, so much so, that I became a 'target.' But even more so, God was showing me something. God was showing me 'the schemes' the enemy had been using to come after me. It is funny because I used to wonder why it was, I always had to do things the hard way. Seemed like nothing ever came easy. Outside of school, things hardly ever came easy for me like it would for other folks. And I never understood why.

Why I had to learn the lessons the 'hard way.' Why it was that it seemed like I could never catch a break. Why it was that someone else could get away with something, but I was always the one who would catch the blame. Until now. God was putting some of the pieces of my life together right there in front of me. You see. When I said that little prayer as a child, God honored it. But the enemy was going to do everything he possibly could to make sure 'that' seed did not grow. Shortly thereafter, I began to endure struggle after struggle after struggle. Until my 'life' issues had grown bigger than my little prayer. I mean, I never fully let go of the prayer or the desire. It just was not at the forefront like I had wanted it to be. And, if the enemy had his way, 'that' seed would never grow to its full potential.

Here is where I was humbled, yet a little confused at first. Because God told me that He was allowing the struggle. He was allowing the mistrust. He was allowing the brokenness. He was allowing the hurt. And I hope you receive this like God told me. Ready? God told me that He allowed everything that has happened in my life to happen because He knew that it would drive me to my knees. And the only way to ignite what He had put on the inside of me was to be driven to my knees. The heartache would cause me to go to my knees. The brokenness would cause me to go to my knees. The mistrust would cause me to go to my knees. The betrayal would cause me to go to my knees. Everything the enemy was trying to use against me to destroy me, God was using it to cause me to go to my knees. And oh, when I got on my knees. It was going to be like fire shut up in my bones (Jeremiah 20:9). 'That' anointing is what the enemy was trying to kill. 'That' anointing is what the enemy was trying to steal away from me. 'That' anointing is what the enemy has been trying to destroy all along (John 10:10). Everything stemmed from a simple confession. Everything stemmed from me using my voice.

And the more and more I did not use my voice, the more I was allowing the enemy to defeat me. As long as I did not know that I was 'Me;' unaware of the seed that God had put on the inside of me, then the enemy was able to continue his tenacious antics of keeping me in the darkness, blind and unaware.

As a child, the enemy bullied me into a corner. Bullied me into keeping quiet. Bullied me by intimidation. Bullied me by guilt. Bullied me by shame. Bullied me into torment. All because he knew that once I got my voice, that would be my weapon. My weapon to expose him for the coward he REALLY is. Now, think about this. The enemy came after a child. A child. When the enemy comes after a child, it has to be 'something' about this child because he pulled out all the stops for a child. But God. He heard my prayer as a little girl, and He knew the warfare I was going to be up against. He knew the enemy would fight me tooth and nail. So no, I understand now why it was that I could not have things coming to me easy. I had to learn how to fight. Spiritually fight. Because I had to draw out what God had put on the inside of me. The moment I spoke up that I was going to be on The Lord's side as a babe, the enemy made me a target. And he did not care that I was only a child. He came at me sometimes subtly. Then, at other times, he came at me with a vengeance. But what he did not expect was for me to come out of that corner swinging.

Swinging for my life back. Swinging for my mind back. Swinging for my marriage back. He underestimated the power of the God inside of me. There is nothing like catching someone off guard. The enemy did not know I was coming out in my Southpaw stance. I surprised him with a jab of forgiveness here. An uppercut of healing there. A right hook of redemption there. A cross of restoration here. A mix of faith and anointing there. Probably the most important "what-nots" I can offer you is to not let the enemy back you in a corner. A corner of guilt or shame. A corner of vulnerability. A corner of depression. A corner of neglect or rejection. Nobody puts Baby in the corner (just a little excerpt from one of my favorite movies, Lone Star State of Mind). Know who you are. Better yet, know Who your God is. And, knowing the enemy he will still come after you. But that is when you have to come out swinging! You have more than you need to come out of whatever you have been through. Your situation. Your choices. Your decisions did not catch God by surprise. He has accounted for your mistakes. He has made provision for your mistakes. God has given you all that you need. Trust me. It is on the inside of you. You just have to tap into it.

For years, I did not understand why it was such a struggle for me to speak. Not just talk. But speak. Speak from my heart. Speak from my emotions. Speak from the innermost part of my being. I wanted to. There was always like a restraint if that makes sense. But the Holy Spirit reminded how the attack on me has always been spiritual (Ephesians 6: 12-13). Being immature, both mentally and spiritually, I always thought my struggle was in my flesh. I thought something was the matter with me. I thought I was the one who was losing it. What I did not know was how to fight spiritually. I must have missed that sermon as a child. But seriously, as long as the enemy could keep me silent, then he could keep me oppressed. Oppressed in my thoughts. Oppressed in my actions. Oppressed in my body. Oppressed in my relationships. Oppressed in my marriage. So initially, that is why 'Perception' ended up becoming my friend. That is why 'Perception' was speaking for me because 'her' voice was louder than my own. And 'her' views spoke volumes over anything I could say. And, sad to say, but Me and 'Perception' stayed playground friends for a while.

Then, God told me that I could sit back and continue to think that 'Perception' was my friend if I wanted to. 'Perception' had been out to devour me.

Looking back, there were quite a few things that could have been resolved with an "easy fix." But now, those "easy fixes" look insurmountable. So many years of not explaining have gone by. So many conversations that were not properly addressed have gone by. So many accusations that never got resolved have gone by. There are so many 'so many's' that it all looks so overwhelming. But God. I am a firm believer that God does not show you something just because. There is a reason for everything. So, when God wakes me up out of my sleep to talk to me, He is trying to show me something kind of like in Jeremiah 33:3, "Ask me and I will tell you remarkable secrets you do not know about things to come." With all that I had been going through in this season, God told me that He allowed life to 'hit me hard' because He had to gracefully break me. Gracefully break me for my purpose. Gracefully break me for what was ahead. Gracefully break me for where He was taking me to. That is why I believe I love the song by Tasha Cobbs Leonard called "Gracefully Broken." Because in one of the lyrics in the song, she testifies how when God breaks you, He does it with such kindness and gentleness. When God breaks you, He does not throw your faults or your predicaments up in your face. When God breaks you, He does not remind you of all of your flaws and mistakes. When God breaks you, He does not condemn you for my ignorance. However, when God breaks you, He shows you the error of your ways with such grace and love. Do I regret some choices I have made in my life? Absolutely. Do I wish I could go back and have a plethora of do-overs? Of course. Do I wish I knew then what I know now? You better believe it. But I cannot. I can only move forward. However, in order to move forward, you cannot keep looking back. I cannot live looking back in regret. I have asked for forgiveness from all my insensitivities. I cannot go back and undo the things I have done. But I can commit that from this day forward, there will not be a repeat cycle.

I have learned so much about myself during this time of my separation. It has literally been a matter of life or death for me. And it was nobody but God that has healed and restored me. I am learning, now, some of the lessons I should have learned years ago. And I hold myself accountable for my part. I am not belittling my past. But I am trying to learn from it. I am trying to accept responsibility from it. I am trying to grow from it. I am trying not to make the same mistakes of yesteryear. I am trying to use the bricks from the wall I tore down to build from. And trust me, I have a lot of steppingstones to build on. I thank God for our "late night" talks because He never fails. And in Him, I am not a failure. I always come out knowing a little more. Learning a little more. Appreciating a little more. Thankful for a little more. Humbled a little more. Healed a little more. Enlightened a little more. Restored a little more. Changed just a little more. I am not there yet where I would like to be. But I am grateful for my "Late Night Friend" that I am not where I used to be.

Now, I take full accountability and responsibility for my actions. I am not perfect, and I have made my fair share of mistakes. But, if the Tena "now" could educate the "then" Tena, I would tell her, "Girl, get it together. And get it together before marriage. Marriage is NOT the time or the place for you to 'grow up.' Being naive to life will not stop the enemy from punkin' you. The same way he goes after seasoned and mature Christians is the same way he goes after babe Christians. He ain't picky on who he seeks to devour. We are all fair game. So, use what your mama gave you! She taught you how to pray. She taught you how to stand on God's Word. She taught you how to have a relationship with God. She taught you how to use the gifts God gave you. She taught you how to speak life and cast down the enemy. She taught you that you always need to be fully clothed in your armor (Ephesians 6: 11-18). She taught you that prayer is your weapon. You are going to have to be on your game because the enemy will certainly be on his. If there is one thing, we can depend on, is that the enemy is always consistent. So, if he is smart enough to know he needs to be consistent, then you need to be the same. Being young does not make you 'off limits' to the enemy. It just makes you more vulnerable if your areas are not covered. There is going to be a book you write called, "From Trial to Test to Testimony... The Promise of Eden." In this book, you will talk about how to cover your areas with prayer. You need to learn how to do this now because you will need to learn how to use your voice to pray. You will need to cover your mind. Your body. Your child(ren). Your finances. Your education. Your marriage. It will be a matter of life or death if you do not learn how to use your weapons. The same prayer that you prayed for God to make you His Servant is the same prayer you pray asking for His Strength. You know God hears your prayers because He lives in you. The enemy is NOT going to take it easy on you because you are a child. He does not care about that. So, girl, you are going to have to LEVEL UP!"

Chapter 14

You are Not Derailed…

Have you ever been praying about one thing and The Spirit leads you down a totally different path? Well, this one morning while I was in prayer, I began praying about one thing. But The Spirit dropped something so heavy on me. You see, I had been battling with capturing my thoughts. Sounds easy enough, huh? It is not. Be fore I began worshipping, however, I was just meditating on why I can sleep so peacefully and restfully. But the minute my body wakes up, my thoughts just begin rolling a mile a minute. I did not understand. So, I was just lying in bed having a conversation with God about this. I did not want my thoughts to be all over the board. But I was having such a difficult time trying to cap ture them. I remembered the verse of how we should capture every thought and make it align to the obedience of Christ (2 Corinthians 10:5). Even though I thought I was doing this, I was still struggling in this area. So, I decided to just get up and pray. And as I was praying about this, God stirred up something else in my spirit. Just follow along. When God stirs something up on the inside of me, He stirs my spirit. He does not stir my thoughts. When my thoughts get stirred up and my mind is going all over the place, that is the spirit of perception trying to take over. God operates in truth NOT perception. That is the en emy trying to convince me to doubt. You see. When God tells us something, we doubt our selves. Or more so, the ability to fulfill that which God told us we could fulfill. We are looking at our own insufficiencies. However, when the enemy tells you something, he is trying to make you doubt God and what He told you. And if he can make you doubt even the slightest, he feels like he is won. That seed of doubt, you do not have to worry about watering, because the enemy will water it for you. He will feed it for you. He will till the ground for you. He will fertilize it for you. Trust me. He will do everything possible to keep you in doubt. The spirit of perception is not from God. That is from the enemy. You have to know God-spirits. And you need to know when spirits are not of God. With the spirit of perception, it is like a high-light reel that just keeps playing over and over in your mind. It shows you your past mistakes. It may show you your flaws. It may show you your vulnerabilities. It may highlight your insecurities. It may highlight your weaknesses. NONE of these things are from God. If you want to know the Spirit of God, read Galatians 5:22-23. And nowhere in that passage, does it mention the confusion that the spirit of perception brings. Nowhere in that passage does it mention the frustration that the spirit of perception brings. Nowhere in that passage does it mention the animosity that the spirit of perception brings. Nowhere in that passage does it mention the anger that the spirit of perception brings. Nowhere in that passage does it mention the betrayal that the spirit of perception brings. Nowhere in that passage does it mention the guilt or shame that the spirit of perception brings. This is NOT the wardrobe of God. Just like you know the names of different designers of things, know your Designer. And if you are not wearing something from God's Line, trust me, it AIN'T going to be a good look.

But getting back to that spirit of perception. I am going to reference the parable of wheat and weeds in Matthew 13:24-30. And to paraphrase, Jesus is talking about how good seed can get deterred from fulfilling its purpose. The very first line of this parable, in verse 24 says, "God's Kingdom is like a man who planted good seed in his field." This "man" the scripture is referring to is God. And the good seed He has planted is us. So, no matter how things may not be looking good in your life right now, GOD SAYS, "YOU ARE STILL GOOD SEED." No matter how you may be feeling right now, GOD SAYS, "YOU ARE STILL GOOD SEED." No matter what the enemy tries to tell you, GOD SAYS, "YOU ARE STILL GOOD SEED." Remember what I said. The enemy tries to make you doubt what God says. But here it is, God is telling you that He has planted you in the earth, in His Field, for a reason. You do have a purpose. And let me show you why I know you have a purpose. Look at verse 25. It says, "That night, while everyone was asleep, the man's enemy came and planted weeds among the wheat and then left." That is the classic M.O. of the enemy. He throws the rock then hides his hand. First off, he came through at night. In the darkness is how he rolls. While everyone was 'asleep.' So, he would go unnoticed. Subtle. Just like a coward. Creeping around in the dark. He planted something that he would hope 'choke' or doubt what God already told you, you are. Then he leaves. Just like a thief! Trying to take something that does not belong to him.

When I was praying that morning, that is when I realized that WE all are good seed. But just because God says we are is not enough sometimes. We have to believe ourselves that we are. And the only way we can believe what God says about us is to receive it by faith. Hence Hebrews 11:6 and James 2:17. But again, if the enemy can make you doubt, by planting seeds of perception in your thoughts, he is won. So, he thinks. The enemy tries to intimidate you into NOT believing what God has told you. The enemy tries to intimidate you into thinking you are seeing something that is not there. The enemy tries to intimidate you into thinking that you did not actually hear what you thought you heard. The enemy tries to intimidate you into thinking you cannot trust 'you.' Let alone God. He goes about to and fro seeking whom he can devour. This IS his job. He does not punch in at 9am and punch out at 5pm. He does not have the weekends off. He does not take FMLA. He does not go on vacation. He IS always here. He IS always trying to stir up doubt, chaos and confusion. And as long as you keep meeting him on the playground at recess, you cannot just stop playing with him because you have found some new friends. No. He does not work like that. He does not know how to take "No" for an answer. So, he becomes this 'stalker-type' friend. Lurking behind every corner. Trying to sit next to you in class. Wanting to ride with you in the front seat. Trying to give you different cooking recipes to try. His job is not done until he makes you doubt.

But wait for it. Wait for it. Wait for it. In verse 29 and 30, the seed (i.e., wheat) and the weeds grow together. Told you. The enemy is

ALWAYS around. Right there. But did you catch that? The seed (i.e., US) and the weeds (i.e., what the enemy plants) grew TOGETHER. That lets me know that no matter what the enemy tries to do, he cannot destroy the seed (i.e., Me). He cannot destroy God's seed! He uses all kinds of measures to stop our growth. But he cannot kill what God has put on the inside of us. Unless we allow him to.

So, as I was praying and God was showing me this revelation, I began to make a declaration over my life that I am good seed. My circumstances do not determine my value. My mistakes do not determine my worth. My insecurities do not determine my insufficiencies. God has given me God-fidence and I know that I can do all things through Christ who strengthens me (Philippians 4: 13). So, when my thoughts want to act like they are out of alignment with what The Word of God says about me, I have to snatch them up and send them back to the pits from whence they came. My seed has purpose. My seed has life. I have an assignment. And I am not willing to compromise any more time than what I have already given. I am destiny-driven because God has put something unique on the inside of me. That is why I cannot be like anyone else. I am not a replica or a duplicate. God has given me unique gifts and talents. And once I mix my faith with the seed that God has planted on the inside of me, my gifts will make room for me. My own lane. My own course. Just for me.

Chapter 15

What-Nots #9

It's Not Just 'Bling Bling'...

I have what you may think is an awkward question for you to think about. When two people become separated, should they still wear their wedding ring? I have pondered this time and time again. But I have never been able to come up with one 'unanimous' answer. So, I have concluded that there is a right or wrong answer. This is solely based on the preference of each per son. So, my answer, you may have a little ambi guity with. But again, this is 'my' answer, and it is 'my' preference. When my husband and I first separated, yes, I did continue to wear my wed ding ring. Outside of it just being part of my nor mal routine for over I 7 years, it just felt right. It had just become a habit I had practiced for so long. However, as the months turned into a year, and months continued to add onto the year, my feelings began to change. And, as far as I was con cerned, we were somewhere in the middle. In the middle because we had not discussed anything about going forward. Whether we were going forward together or separately, there was no finite resolution. Whether that change was talk ing and going to counseling or meeting up at an attorney's office to discuss options. The more we did not talk, the more frustrated, angrier, and de feated I would become. All because I did not see any sign of change during this very cold and iso lated season. So, with all these factors being in place, this should have made the inclination eas ier to not wear my wedding ring, right? Well, let me tell you. I did try to stop wearing my wedding ring. On more than one occasion. But, let me tell you about this specific instance I remember like it happened this morning. While heading out the door one morning on my way to work, I inten tionally left my ring in the jewelry box. Thinking I was 'grown' and could do what I wanted to do I was purposeful in my actions. And, when I was turning the key to lock my door, I caught view of my hand. And in that exact moment, I was quick ened and convicted. God did not say a single word. All God showed me was a glimpse of something I acted like I had left on accident. Something I had knowinglyforgotten. In this glimpse, God showed me a vision of the exact place where my wedding ring was positionally located in my jewelry box. So, in my puzzlement, I walked back inside to retrieve my item. My wedding ring. I got it. And I slipped it on my finger and just continued with going about my day; not really putting too much thought into it my 'morning experience.' However, there was a lot God was waiting to 'call me to the carpet' regarding the whole experience. Regarding myfeelings. Regarding my lovely attitude. I do not remember the timeline from my 'morning experience' to when God spoke. But, when He did, I got called to the carpet like I thought. In my defense to God, my first rebuttal, or explanation, was that in my state of confusion, why did 'I' have to still honor my marriage? I do not even talk to my husband. The only marriage we have is on paper. I went on and on and on. And when I had finished explaining, God calmly asked me if I was done? And I am going to tell you just how it was told to me. Again, God took me back to a chapter in my other book, "From Trial to Test to Testimony...The Promise of Eden." And the chapter is entitled, "Are Your Areas Covered?" Well, in this particular chapter, I talk about how you have to keep your areas covered with prayer. And one of those areas was marriage. And God gave me a deeper meaning pertaining to the visual 'representation' of marriage. And one visual 'representation' of marriage is the 'symbolization,' or presence, of a ring. The wedding ring that I so hastily wanted to stop wearing. That was the 'symbolization' of my covering. The covering for my marriage. That ring is my shield. That ring reminds that I should not be entertaining the sly and sneaky tricks of the enemy. That ring is my reminder that in my own weakness, God's strength is made upright in my vulnerabilities. Every time I looked at that ring, I was reminded to be praying for covering because the enemy does not play fair. That ring reminds me to cover my area---my marriage. We all know how conniving the enemy can be. We all know how subtle the enemy can be. But, even with all his efforts against you, against your marriage, when you look down at your finger and see your covering, you are not giving the enemy any room to wiggle his way into that area.

But, even knowing all this, I still have had the urge to stop wearing my wedding ring. Not because I do not love my husband and want my marriage to reconcile. But because I do not see any change. Actually, things look like a valley of dry bones. Bones that have no desire to want to be revived. Bones that have no desire to want to be resurrected. Although I try to stay upbeat and encouraged, it is a struggle. This has truly been the absolute hardest thing I have ever had to deal with. And I will be honest. I have wanted to just quit and throw in the towel. I have wanted to just have this marriage over and done with. But no sooner than I would have the thought, I would get convicted. And I never really understood why. Then my lightbulb moment. One night while I was talking to a friend of mine, I asked her to pray for me and my husband. To my surprise, she told me she does. And in actuality, she fasts one day a week and always includes us in her fast. Here it was, this girl was showing her faith in action by fasting for me and I was at the point of wanting to quit. After inquiring a little more about her fast, I decided to join her. Because some recent 'findings' had just come to the surface, this could not have come at a better time. So, I fasted. All that morning, I heard nothing. All that afternoon, silence. And then right before I was getting ready for bed, God gave me some instructions. The first thing God told me to do was to stop speaking death over the atmosphere (Proverbs 18:21). For I was going to get just what I was speaking. Then God told me to never make a permanent decision out of a temporary emotion. No matter how I felt. No matter the level of communication. No matter what was going on. No matter what picture the enemy was trying to paint. Remember, the enemy is the father of lies (John 8:44). He is the master of deception (Daniel 8:25). Your perception only becomes a reality as you continue to feed into it. So, stop giving it life!

At the end of the day, God told me that all of the "no matter's" did not matter. The things we see are only temporary. So, look to God for all things eternal (2 Corinthians 4: 18). Do not lose sight of Him. Do not take your focus off of Him. Do not get bamboozled by what "you think you see." God said that the enemy was using the same old trick of perception to try and defeat me. The game does not change. Just the players. And this time, the enemy was trying to make 'Me' the key player. The one thing I had to recall was that every promise that God made to me, the enemy was right there to discourage me that it would not come to pass. But truthfully, that is his job. He is there to make you doubt God and His Word. To make you not walk in faith. And if you do not walk in faith, then it is impossible for you to please God (Hebrews 11:6). So, his sole purpose is to get you out of alignment with God's order. Because he is your #1 Accuser to God. So, if your choices are outside of the promises of God, you better tread lightly. Because the enemy will lead you down a road so far that you end up wandering alone aimlessly.

When I was contemplating not wearing my wedding ring, I can be honest, I was only trying to validate my reasoning out of frustration. I was only trying to validate my reasoning out of exhaustion. I was only trying to validate my reasoning out of unsettledness. I was only really contemplating this action because I felt like we were at the point of no return. As God convicted me, He reminded me that my vow was to Him first. So, I kept wearing my ring because of what it meant to God and because of what the commitment meant to me. Think about it like this. If you are a school crossing guard and rain is predicted in the forecast for that day. How do you prepare for what is anticipated to come? You may wear your raincoat, your rain boots, your rain hat, and your umbrella. You prepare and clothe yourself to protect from what you believe is headed your way. Well, the same is true in marriage and wearing your wedding ring. Me choosing not to wear it put me at a greater risk of being naked and exposed. Exposing myself to unwanted, or wanted, advances. Exposing myself in my vulnerabilities. Exposing myself in my weaknesses. When you have been separated from your spouse for so long, you are going to get weak. And whatever your weak area is may be totally different from mine. But bottom line, you will get weak. Not wearing my wedding ring made me more susceptible to entertaining these advances that I would have otherwise ignored. I did not want the attention from a stranger. I did not want the advances from the guy opening my door at Starbucks. I did not want the attention from one of my patients at work. My ring was my covering. My ring was my reminder of what I wanted. My ring was my reminder of who I had made a vow to in the presence of. My ring was my reminder of who I had committed to in the presence of. My ring was my reminder of what and who I loved. Attention from others may be innocent, but that is not who I wanted the attention and the advances from. I wanted it from my husband. I kept wearing my ring because of what I wanted. What I still expected God to do in my marriage. What I still hoped God would do in my marriage. What I still believed God would do in my marriage.

God condones marriage and the promises that it brings. And if God condones it, you have officially become a target for the enemy. So, outside of treading lightly over perception, I would say more importantly "what-nots" to do is making permanent decisions stemming from temporary and sometimes misunderstood feelings. I understand feelings are strong and they feel right. But they do not last forever. They do change. They can change. So, do not ever get too caught up in the "emotions" of things that you cannot see the bigger picture. Remember your vows. And, if you cannot remember your vows, remember the vows that God created for your marriage in Mark 10:9, "Because God created this organic union of the two sexes, no one should desecrate his art by cutting them apart." Marriage is artwork that God created. So, do not always be so quick to desecrate or destroy the masterpiece that God has created between you and your spouse. When you put your marriage on the line, and expose its emotional vulnerabilities, the enemy will make you feel, or make you see, just what you are looking for. Trust me, he will. So, be careful of the decisions you make out of what you think you see. Be careful of the decisions you make out of your feelings. And if you get to the point where it is hard to separate your feelings from truth, ask God to show you His. Your truth can change. Your spouse's truth can even change. The truth of the situation may even change. But God's truth will never change (Hebrews 13:8). That is the truth you base your relationship on. That is the truth that you base your marriage on. That is the truth you base your life on. That is the truth you stand on.

Always go back to God's Word. He has provided so many 'reassurances' to help us along our journey. But one of my favorites is found in Philippians 1:6 and it states, "For I am confident of this very thing, that He who began a good work in you will perfect it until the day of Christ Jesus." We are all imperfect and we will all make mistakes. But the only thing that covers our imperfectness is God's perfect love.

Today, there is not a second thought about whether or not I wear my covering. No. My circumstances have not changed. And yes, my husband and I are still estranged. But my obedience is to God at his point. Whatever He tells me to do, I will do. Whatever He tells me to wear, I will wear. Will I look foolish? Probably. Will I look crazy. No doubt. But, if my obedience to God makes me look a little silly, then I will just be silly. Because the one thing I know, God predestined me. God called me. God will justify me. And God will glorify me (Romans 8:30). This is meant with the utmost sincerity and tactfulness. But I am past the point of being a 'people' pleaser. Been there. Done that. Got a whole closet full oft-shirts. I do not just want to make 'good' decisions. I intentionally want to make God decisions. And yes. There is a difference between good decisions versus God decisions. Bottom line: not all good decisions are God-based. So, you have to be careful of the 'real' motivation behind some of your choices. As I strive to make God decisions, I am aligning my will to God's will. I am aligning my ways to God's ways. I am aligning my path to God's path for my life. So, whatever journey God has for my life, I know I can trust Him. I will not become bitter waiting. I will not become angry waiting. I will not become frustrated waiting. I will not get tired waiting. I will not be disheartened waiting. The waiting is where your faith is tested. The waiting is where your perseverance is tried. The waiting is where you are made fire-proof. Just remember that in the waiting room, God promises Isaiah 40:31, "But those who hope in the Lord will renew their strength. They will soar on wings like eagles; they will run and not grow weary; they will walk and not be faint." God also promises in Galatians 6: 9, "And let us not grow weary of doing good, for in due season we will reap, if we do not give up." It is tough but wait for it. It is uncomfortable but wait for it. It may be 'complicated,' but God says, "Wait for it. Your efforts and your labor will not be in vain (1 Corinthians 15:58)."

Now, while you are waiting, there will be things that come up against your faith. But the one thing God told me was that faith is required during times of trouble, not feelings. I could not have put that "what-nots" better myself. If we would all remember that as we are going through, imagine how we could shut the enemy down when we see him at the door? Because the one thing God never said was that we would not have trouble. But trouble does not have to have us. Another "what-nots" is to look at things perpetually and not through perception. God is perpetual; meaning He is never-ending. He is never changing. He is everlasting. He is eternal. He is permanent. Something perpetual remains the same. Regardless of the circumstances. Regardless of the situation. Regardless of people. Regardless of anything. God's truth is perpetual. Unlike our truth. That is why you do not make decisions out of 'your truth.' That is why you do not make decisions out of 'your perception.' As you have heard before, perception is temporary. Perception is ever-changing. Perception is only a belief. Perception is variable. Perpetualism is absolute. That is why I strive to make God decisions. Because my natural eyes have limited vision and can only see so far. My own eyes have deceived me before. So, I know my own eyes will deceive me about someone else. My natural vision is variable because it changes. But, through God's spiritual eyes, His vision is all-seeing, and He will show me all that He wants me to see. God will show me the 'heart' of people and not the 'perception' of them that the enemy tries to show me.

Chapter 16

What-Nots #10

Couch-Time Is Sometimes Needed...

I hope this does not come off the wrong way because I mean this with the utmost sincerity. But I can only speak of things that I have experi enced. Paths and journeys that I have walked. There is a stigma associated with needing help. It does not make you look weak. It does not make you immature. It does not make you look like you cannot handle things. It does not make you look like any of these things. All it makes you look like, is that you need help. Do not be afraid to reach out when it is needed. From my experience, some people do not necessarily feel comfortable reaching out for help. First off, we do not like people in our business. What happens at home, stays at home. It is not anybody's busi ness what is going on behind my doors or under your roof. If you stay out of mine, then I can mind my own. Secondly, few of us like to admit when we are wrong. It is one thing to know you are wrong. But it is another thing when someone tells you that you are wrong. Why would you ex pose yourself to a double whammy? Never. We are, and get, so stuck in our ways that even when we know we need to bend, we do not because we just have to have things go our way. All I can say is, keep on with that attitude. And hit me up in a few years and tell me where that has gotten you. Thirdly, some of us have a little too much pride and we want to make everyone think that all of our ducks are nicely lined up in a row. But truth be told. Half of us probably cannot even.find our ducks to line up. But you will never know that. And lastly, and probably the most comical, is that we do not want to pay for no help. Seeking outside help is such a waste of money. Half the folks trying to tell you how to get things in order in your life are half crazy as well. And you want me to pay them for their advice? What possibly could you be smoking on my friend? That ain't happening captain. No way. No how. After all the excuses have been used up. After all the explanations have been exhausted. Then what? Do you still have the same problems? Have they left yet? Have the issues been resolved? Has the relationship gotten any better? Or is it stagnant and feels like it is not going anywhere? So, what is your resolve? What are you willing to do to help the situation? What compromises are you willing to try in order to promote life in your marriage instead of death? Any suggestions? I am listening. I am open to all suggestions.

While I am waiting on your suggestion, I want to share with you what I tried. And before I share with you my journey, let me first tell you. The only reason I can offer the earlier excuses is because I have used them all to some form of degree. I never really was against counseling until I actually went. There have been a few times that my husband and I went to counseling. And can I be honest? I was a little reluctant, but I went. After the first counselor basically pointed the finger at me at being the "cause" of what we were going through, from that point on, I was done. How dare him? I did not want to go in the first place. And now, you telling me, our issues are all my fault? Whether it was or not, I felt attacked. ations have been exhausted. Then what? Do you still have the same problems? Have they left yet? Have the issues been resolved? Has the relationship gotten any better? Or is it stagnant and feels like it is not going anywhere? So, what is your resolve? What are you willing to do to help the situation? What compromises are you willing to try in order to promote life in your marriage instead of death? Any suggestions? I am listening. I am open to all suggestions.

While I am waiting on your suggestion, I want to share with you what I tried. And before I share with you my journey, let me first tell you. The only reason I can offer the earlier excuses is because I have used them all to some form of degree. I never really was against counseling until I actually went. There have been a few times that my husband and I went to counseling. And can I be honest? I was a little reluctant, but I went. After the first counselor basically pointed the finger at me at being the "cause" of what we were going through, from that point on, I was done. How dare him? I did not want to go in the first place. And now, you telling me, our issues are all my fault? Whether it was or not, I felt attacked.

So, any counselors after that, I was not really trying to hear. That first instance had put a nasty taste in my mouth. So, it just made it easier to quit before I even tried. It made it easier to be defensive before I heard any word that came out of their mouth. It just made it easier for our issues to continue going on unresolved. It just made it easier for the seeds that the enemy had already planted to just continue to grow.

To my surprise, when my husband and I separated, it was 'Me' who suggested counseling. I believed this to be the last attempt of restoring our marriage. I knew this time going to counseling would be different. And I knew that because I was different. During my separation, I was changing. God was changing me. God was healing me. God was restoring me. And this time, I just knew the experience would be different. What I did not realize then that I knew now, was that I had not yet met the 'real' me. The person I was, was not the 'real' me. The 'real' me that God showed me I was. But, when I would have my "mirror experience," all things changed. There was no more hiding my weaknesses. There was no more 'putting on fronts.' There was more trying to cover up my insecurities. There was no more trying to overshadow my vulnerabilities. There was no more being opaque or blurry. My exposure in the "mirror experience" led to me being transparent before God. And in that transparency, I was able to stand in my truth. I was able to own my truth. And glory to God, that in 'that' truth, God could work with 'that' truth.

All the other attempts at counseling, we were putting what we believed to be our needs first. Our needs as far as what we wanted or expected from the other person. But what we should have been doing was seeking God first for His direction. And as we put God in His place first, then I believe that He would not only have shown us what the other person needed, but He would have also shown us how to supply those needs. So yes, this time, my mindset was not about me or even my husband. This time, everything was all about God. This time, God would tell us how He wanted to be glorified through our marriage. This time, God would show us how to use our marriage to get His Glory. This time, God would use our marriage as a demonstration of what He can do if only we would trust Him. All the times before, we were only trying to 'satisfy' our own needs and not God's needs through us. And yes, I do believe that God will satisfy our needs according to His riches and glory. But let us not forget we have to qualify ourselves. Because everyone is not eligible. We have to invite Him into our lives. Into our marriage. So, this time, my expectation was different. It was not in my husband. It definitely was not in myself. It was not even in the counselor. I mean we all have a different part to play in order to create the beautiful sound coming from this symphony called marriage. But, truthfully, my expectation was (is) in God. I was ready to put God first. I was ready to 'let go' of those things I never really had control of. I was ready to let God use me, and my marriage, in the magnitude that He intended for it to be all along. All the times before, we were looking at each other to be 'fixed' and not leaving any room for God to step in and 'fix' those areas that He wanted to heal. So, this time, I believed wholeheartedly, it would be different. I was finally looking to God to do the healing. I was finally looking to God to do the restoring. I was finally looking to God to do the repairing. I was finally looking for God to do what He had intended all along. I was finally ready to put God in His rightful place, at the head of my life and at the head of my marriage.

When God puts two people together, and hence, I did say when "God" puts two people together, He has an ordained purpose for the marriage. No one can convince me that my marriage was not God-ordained. And I know that because God gave us purpose. God gave us an assignment. God gave us an ordination to fulfill. I just did not realize it then. Sure, when my husband and I got together, I was mature in age. But my mindset was nowhere near being mature. I still had a lot of emotional, mental, and spiritual growth to do. In essence, I was still Growing Up In Marriage ... Perfectly Flawed. Yall, I had no idea how much baggage I was bringing into my marriage. So no, I was not ready for no counseling. I had not grown up yet. In my defense, I did not know who I was. So, how could I honestly expect my husband to know who I was or what I needed? The struggle was real for me. But it did not start in my marriage. The side effects just showed up in my marriage. In my naivety, I made the enemy's 'hit list' many years ago. But, as my relationship with God deepened and the more, I listened, the more He spoke. And I was now understanding why the struggle for me was so intense. I was now understanding why the wall around my heart was a barrier. I was now understanding why the strong-hold over my mind was so relentless. My staying in the dark allowed the enemy to keep his 'hook' in me. Because he knew once I cried out for help, God would be right there. And that would me that he would get exposed. He would get exposed as the liar he is (John 8:44). He would get exposed as the deceiver he is (Daniel 8:25). He would get exposed as the thief he is (John 10:10). Yep, the enemy had me trapped. And, for a long time. But I am no longer in the dark. I am no longer trapped by my past. I am no longer a slave to my mistakes. I am no longer in bondage to my sins. The enemy knew God would free me. And God did just that. But I had to be willing to do my part. And that was being as totally candid and transparent as I could be. Change comes from truth, right? Well, this is my transparent truth. This is my transparent truth that I live in every day. This is my transparent truth that I cannot change. This is my transparent truth that I own. This is my transparent truth that I am taking accountability for. This is my transparent truth in which I have to live with the consequences I have caused.

And before I begin opening up about this decision, I need you to understand that I struggled with this option. I struggled with the embarrassment from my past mistakes. I struggled with the shame of some of my past choices. I struggled with all the guilt that I slept with every night. I was a 'hot mess.' But then the Holy Spirit convicted me and gave me this illustration. When you are not feeling well, we go see the doctor. When you find yourself in legal trouble, you go see an attorney. When you want something to eat, you go to a restaurant. When your pipes flood your kitchen, you call a plumber. Do you not know that God strategically places people at different steps in our path for our use? All for Him to get the Glory? There was absolutely no logical reason that I could come up with that would satisfy me not going. So, I did it. I finally decided to give counseling a try, on my own. And wouldn't you know it? I was able to get an appointment the very next day. I was nervous. Yet, I was a little excited. Excited because this time, I knew I was ready because this time counseling was not just about me. It was about me surrendering to how God wanted to use me in my marriage. In my life. In my purpose. I was ready and willing to allow God to show me what my husband needed from me in our marriage. Not whole-heartedly focusing on what I thought my husband needed or even what he thought he needed. I was ready to become a servant of love unto God to meet those needs that He has ordained me to meet. Let me explain. I have always had a serving mindset and I believe in The Word that when you humble yourself and serve others, God will bless you (1 Peter 4:10). God will exalt you (1 Peter 5:6). I believe that as you serve others, God will not only provide your needs, but He also gives you the desires of your heart. So, you do not always have to think your needs should be in the limelight or the focus of your marriage. Serve God and He will supply all your needs according to His riches in glory (Philippians 4:19). Truthfully, going to counseling by myself was quite intimidating. For whatever reason, I saw going to a counselor is like a sign of defeat. A sign of weakness if you will. For a lot of us, we are taught that we do not need any help and if you ask for help, then something is wrong with you. But that is so far from the truth. Yes, we were taught to be strong. Yes, we were taught to be independent. Yes, we were taught to not have to depend on other folks. Yes, we were taught that vulnerability equals weakness. And yes, we were taught to be self-sufficient. But, even in The Word it talks about the advantages of helping one another, "Two are better than one, because they have a good reward for their toil. For if they fall, one will lift up his fellow. But woe to him who is alone when he falls and has not another to lift him up (Ecclesiastes 4:9-1 O)!" We are here to help lift up, encourage, and support one another. But as long as you think that you always have to walk alone. As long as you think you have to get through the tough times on your own. As long as you think you can always handle things on your own, you are giving room for the enemy to deceive you and keep you in darkness. You are allowing the enemy to keep that stronghold around your neck. Around your heart. Around your mind. And he does not let up until you give up. And maybe like me, you need to 'refresh' your thoughts from your old way of thinking. I had to 'refresh' my thoughts to get into alignment with how God wants me to live. And He wants me to live free. He wants me to live joyous. He wants me to live peacefully. He wants me to live liberated. He wants me to live not in bondage. He wants me to live stronghold-free! So, for my own peace of mine, if I did not do anything else, I knew just been exposed to so much during this time of my separation. I had been shown a plethora of hurts. A plethora of pains. A plethora of traumas. A plethora of mistakes. A plethora of flaws. A plethora of sins at how I had been living my life. Past and present. And I was not willing to carry these little 'charms' into my future. It was during this time of separation, that I was dealing with the effects of some 'pains' that had happened in my life. I was dealing with the effects of getting molested. I was dealing with the effects of not getting what I needed from my biological father to feel valuable, worthy and loved. I was dealing with the effects of being bullied. I was dealing with the effects of why I had compartmentalized all my hurts and pains for years. And it left me without a voice. I am not glad I separated. But honestly, if I had not separated, 1do not know ifI would have addressed all these little 'charms' that were in my pandora box. But needless to say, I was trying to move forward in my life. But I just needed a little help in doing so. That is when I decided to go seek help. And for me, that was a HUGE step. But, after getting there and just talking with the counselor, it actually helped. And you know what else I liked? There was no judgement or condemnation when I told my truth. I did not have to put on a front. I did not have to act like I was the victim. I did not have to act like all my choices had been right. I just talked. I just told my truth. I owned my truth. I made myself accountable for my truth. And now, I am living in the consequences of my truth. And I do not know if this is common or not, but after our session(s), my counselor prayed. And they do not just pray for me. But they pray for my husband, my marriage, my child, my family, my life. That was different for me. But a good different. This was my first experience of counseling not being condescending.

And I believe a lot of that has to do with 'me.' I had grown up. I was different. God was transforming me right before my eyes. So now, I am changing my mind about counseling. There were so many different factors that pushed me to give this a chance. But, I know, God was at the center of it all.

As a wife, God created me to be my husband's help meet (Genesis 2: 18). And, if you are confused about what a help meet is, let me clarify it for you. A help meet is a helpful companion or partner, ESPECIALLY one's husband or wife. You are there to help encourage them. You are there to support them. You are there to uplift them. You are there to embrace and care for them. You are your spouse's rib. You are their legs when they cannot walk. You are their eyes when they cannot see. You are there to be their ears when they cannot hear. You are there to comfort when they need a shoulder to lean on. You are there to love them; unconditionally and unblemished. You are there to help your spouse meet the need that God has destined for your marriage. However, if God is not first in this equation, things can become so entangled. Things can be come so misconstrued. Things can become so misunderstood. Things can become so "perceptionalized" (i.e., this is my own definition when a person's perception becomes their reality. And since it is their perception and this perception has become their reality, this has become their truth).

To God be the glory that my mistakes of yesteryear, was just that, the past. Yes, I had made them, but I could not get stuck there. Yes, I had made them, but I could not let them define my future. Yes, I had made them, but I could not continue to live my life riddled with guilt. I had been given a gift. New revelation. New truth. A new mindset with new expectations. And it all came from God. God's desires were going to be met in my marriage this time. God's joy was going to reside in my marriage this time. God's peace was going to overtake our minds this time. God's love was going to overflow from us this time. This time, and call me crazy, and sometimes it does take crazy faith, but I am that crazy one who is crazy enough to believe that NOTHING is impossible with God (Luke 1:37). Believe it or not, God really does know what we need. And He can supply our needs so much better than we can supply for ourselves (Philippians 4:19). For

He knows our beginning before our ending (Isaiah 46:10). For it was God that numbered the hairs on our head (Luke 12:7). For it is God who knew the plans for you before you were formed in your mother's womb (Jeremiah 29:11). Everything will ALWAYS go back to God. So, let go of your grip and stop letting the enemy have free reign in your marriage. By faith, turn it over to God and let God repair those damaged fences. Turn it over to God and let Him mend the broken bridges. Turn it over to God and let Him fill those empty holes. Turn it over to God and let Him restore your mind, body, and soul. Turn things over to God and let Him do Him. Trust me, He is good at it!

As I was praying one morning, I decided to open my blinds. I rarely do that because I like a quiet dark space to pray. But this morning was different. I was unctioned to let some 'light' into the 'dark' space I was in. Selah. Well, this particular morning, my heart was a little heavy because of something I had been dealing with the day before. There was like a 'real' battle going on in my mind. And I knew why. But nevertheless, the enemy was being just that---the enemy. So, in prayer that morning, I was particularly seeking God's presence in the situation. As I was in the midst of praying, I began to see snow flurries outside. This may not sound like a big deal, but in the part of Texas where I lived, it was a big deal. That does not happen often. At least, not that I have seen. I immediately stopped praying and just began crying as I watched the snow flurries scatter throughout the air. I do not know why I was so emotional, but I could not stop praising God. Praising God that He allowed me to witness this. Praising God that He is so miraculous. Praising God for the season that I was yet in. Almost like my season was changing right before my eyes. And even it was only for a brief moment, before the snow flurries disappeared onto the ground, I 'saw it.' God had shown it to me. As I started back praying, one of the things I remember asking God for was to protect me from the spirit of deception. I wanted a deeper discernment to know God's Word. To be able to stand on God's truth. If it was not God's truth, then it was a lie. And I wanted to no longer get deceived by the enemy. And as I was praying, almost immediately, the snow flurries fell in my spirit. And God shared something so powerful with me during prayer. God told me that He had given me a 'natural' glimpse of The

Word coming to life. The Word that God talks about in Hebrews 11:1, "Now faith is the substance of things hoped for, the evidence of things not seen." God said that He had given me a glimpse of what faith looks like to Him (in the spirit). God said, "When I make you a promise, I show it to you in the spirit first. Your faith, and its activation, is what makes your spiritual promise manifest in the natural realm. Just like there was no evidence of the snow flurries that were hitting the ground, but you saw it falling. That is how I desire you to receive My Word in the Spirit. I show you things in the spirit so that you will continually keep saying what you saw until you see what you have been saying. They that worship Me must worship me in spirit and in truth (John 4:24). That is why I show you things in the spirit first. It is up to you to hold onto the promises I have given you. Believe that your faith will activate the promises of what I have already shown you. When I allow you to 'see' in the spirit (the substance of things hoped for), you are to hold onto what you saw (now faith), until you see in the natural (evidence of things not seen) what I have shown you in the spirit." When God told me that, I began crying some more. Crying in joy because all the time, you do not see the natural manifestation of what God has shown you in the spirit. Crying in joy because all the time, the enemy tries to convince you that what God showed you will not come to pass. Crying in joy because all the time, you may not even be sure that what you heard was even God. But God told me that if He showed it to you, then by faith, it is yours. Then I began to understand Matthew 11:12 a little better. Just because God promises you something, does not mean that you won't have to 'do the work' to get it. And the work is activating your faith. If we (Christians) are the kingdom, and the kingdom suffers violence (i.e., deception, doubt, fear, worry, lack, abuse, anxiety, depression, etc....), the violent (Christians) have to take what was ours back by force. Because the enemy is not just going to give you back your peace. The enemy is not just going to give you back your joy.

The enemy is not just going to give you back your mind. You are going to have to spiritually fight to take back those things that God said is yours.

So, whatever God has promised you, it belongs to you. Just like there was no evidence of snow flurries on the ground, I saw them when they were falling. That is how we, as Christians, should hold onto the things of God. When God shows you something, no matter what our natural eyes see, you have to say, no devil, I saw it. No matter what our circumstances may or may not look like, you have to say, no devil, I saw it. You have to hold onto what God showed you with faith. Otherwise, the enemy will deceive you out of what already belongs to you. So yeah. That day, God did not just answer the prayer that was in my heart. But He gave me a revelation to apply to my life. I serve a God that is more than able to do exceedingly, abundantly, above all I could ever think or ask; according to the power (i.e., faith) that worketh in us (Ephesians 3:20).

So, the "what-nots" God gave me was to not let the enemy steal what does not belong to him. God's Kingdom lives on the inside of each and every one of us. And, we have to protect what is ours. Do not let the enemy convince you that God is not real. Do not let the enemy punk you out of your blessings. Do not let the enemy deceive you from believing that God does not want the best for His children. Half the battle is in your mind. However, once you capture those thoughts and make them come into alignment with the Word of God (2 Corinthians 10:5), he has lost. If what your mind is telling is not God's truth, then those thoughts are a lie. And they are not of God. They are from the master deceiver (Daniel 8:25). So, send them back to hell where they came from.

If I could give a few more "what-nots" from the 'new' Tena to the 'old' Tena, I would tell her not to shut down the idea of new possibilities. Do get so complacent that you miss out on new opportunities to learn something. To grow. To develop. To enhance. Do not live your life in your 'feelings.' Feelings are temporary. But God's truth is eternal, and it is what you will need to stand on (2 Corinthians 4:18). Everything else in your life will crumble if God is not your foundation. You will have to learn how to build your faith and it is IMPOSSIBLE to please God without faith (Hebrews 11 :6). Stay open and know 'Who' your life, your marriage represents. Your marriage is bigger than you. It is bigger than your husband. Your marriage is a vow of honor

121

to God. If you put God first, I promise He will add to you. He will add to your marriage. He will add to your life in immeasurable ways. Trust Him.

For far too long, I have let my past and my past mistakes keep me in bondage. We have all probably heard the story of Jacob and Esau around Genesis 25. But, this time, God gave me 'fresh' revelation. And I am going to paraphrase just a bit. Jacob and Esau were twins. And even in the womb, they were at odds. Jacob was always snapping at his older brother's Esau's heels. And, throughout Jacob's whole life, he spent it being a deceiver. He spent his life going after things that belonged to other people. He spent his life always trying to 'come up' on folks the back-handed kind of way. Basically, at someone else's expense and on someone else's dime. His name, Jacob, actually means deceitful. Later on, in life, Jacob was able to trick his older brother Esau out of his birthright; twice. And even after he got what he wanted; he still was not happy with the blessing. He was not fulfilled with this 'newfound' blessing. However, over time, the the tension between Jacob and Esau grew. Jacob knew he was wrong for what he had done and unsurprisingly, he became afraid for his life. So, he fled. And, for years. The same kind of deceptive seeds that Jacob had sown was the same kind of harvest he was yet going to receive (i.e., read about Laban, Rachel, and Leah starting in Genesis 29). The same way Jacob used to deceive is the same way he was now getting deceived. Anyway, after some years, Jacob desired to return home to apologize to his brother Esau. Long story short, Jacob wanted to make amends with not just Esau. But he wanted to make amends with all those people he had deceived. Whether it was knowingly or unknowingly. Jacob needed and desired to now own his truth. He needed and desired to now live in his truth. He needed and desired to now take accountability for his actions. To Jacob's surprise, his brother Esau held no grudge against him. And he did forgive his brother, Jacob. But the part that was 'fresh' for me was the revelation of Jacob's encounter with an 'angel' in Genesis 32:22-32. Whether he knew it was an 'angel' or not, he knew it was something different about this man. There was something different about this encounter. And when Jacob told the angel, "I am not going to let you go until you bless me," lets me know that Jacob was ready for a change. Which is why I believe WWE even took place.

Now, I have heard this story time and time again. But it was this time that God gave me 'fresh' revelation. Jacob knew how he was. He could not forget it because his name constantly reminded him of his 'nature.' But that night, I believe Jacob wanted a change. Jacob wanted to be different. Jacob wanted to be healed of his past. Jacob was finally ready to not let his name be his identity. Jacob was finally ready to take the mask off and be who God has called him to be. Jacob was ready to admit and own his truth. And I believe that when God saw Jacob's heart, He knew he was ready. This is the truth God is looking for. This is the truth that God can work with. This is the truth that delivers. This is the truth that restores. This is the truth that heals. This is the truth that changed Jacob's name. Jacob was finally ready to heal from his truth. And it was in this truth, that Jacob was ready to have his "mirror experience." It was in this truth, that Jacob's name was changed. God now called him 'Israel,' which means Triumphant with God or Wrestles with God(Genesis 32:28). And then mylightbulb moment: Jacob was me and I was he! I had been deceitful. Deceitful with my heart. Deceitful with my actions. Deceitful with my loved ones. Deceitful with my love. But, when I had my "mirror experience," and I saw that person staring back at me with that mask on, I knew it was time to own my truth. Before, I was not able to live in my truth because I had not quite realized or acknowledged my truth. But, from that day forward, my name was not Jacob (Tena) anymore. God called me Israel because for years I had been wrestling with Him and what He was calling me to. For years, I had been wrestling in my relationships. For years, I had been wrestling in my marriage. For all the wrestling I had done, I had the belt! But guess what? Do you know why God called Jacob, Israel? Because Israel is a name of victory. Israel is a name of triumph. Genesis 32:28 says it best, "You have wrestled with God and with men, and you have won." Do yall see that? At the end, just as God says Jacob wins, so do I. Do you know how encouraging that is, especially going through a separation? Do you know how encouraging that is, especially when the enemy is constantly trying to give you a "deviated" perception of things? Do you know how encouraging that is, especially when you do not see things changing around you? Do you know how encouraging that is, especially when you are being constantly reminded that you have already lost? Do yall see the joy in my name change? When I heard this, tears rolled down my cheeks. Because at times, I do not feel God's presence. And I certainly do not see God working in my situation. But this here. This was HUGE for me. This let me know that I can keep moving forward. This let me know that God STILL does have my back. This let me know that NOTHING happens to me outside of God's Will. Even when the enemy tries to trick me into thinking that he is in charge. This let me know that I can rest in peace in knowing that God is STILL mindful of me (Psalm 8:4). Go figure. I am on God's mind. So, no matter what I go through, the good work that He started in me, He will finish it (Philippians 1:6). From receiving this blessing from God that day, I am being healed through my 'Jacob-ness.' I am being restored through my 'Jacob-ness.' I am being delivered through my 'Jacob-ness.' From me owning and standing in my truth, God is blessing me, even now, through my 'Jacob-ness.' So now when people try to call me what I used to be. So now, when people try to keep me stuck in the decisions I have made in the past. So now, when people try to remind me and strong-hold me into thinking that God has not changed my heart and my will, I have to stand firm. Nobody knows my 'wrestling' experience. So, I cannot expect no one to appreciate it. Some folks may not believe or even want to "see" the new you. Some of the hardest folks to convince are those that knew you when. When you were in your sin. When you were in your mistakes. When you were enjoying being in your flesh. When you were doing probably the same thing that they are still doing. But rest assured. You just keep being Israel. You do not slow down. You let them catch up. It is not always good to answer by what people call you. Make them call you by name. The name God gave you. So, when you see me and I do not answer, please do not get offended. I am just trying not to get pulled back to that person I used to be. I am trying to walk in the authority that God has given me.

So, if you want to know a little about me, here it goes. Hi, my government name is Tena. But somewhere along my journey, God renamed me to Israel. Why Israel you say? Because Israel is a chain-breaker. Israel is a freedom seeker. Israel fought to give God all he had. Israel received beauty for all his scars. Israel owned his truth. Israel wanted something different for his life. Israel lived the rest of his life trying to please God. Israel is me. Please to make your acquaintance.

The enemy has punked me for far too long trying to convince me of this or trying to convince me of that. But here and no further. Anything that God has promised me, I am going after it because it is mine. The enemy tried to convince me years ago that counseling was a joke. But, oh I declare, he was such a liar. The enemy tried to convince me years ago that no one would ever love me because of what I have done and what I have been through. But au contraire. He is such a liar. The enemy tried to convince me that my child would always be astray. But, au contraire, he is such a liar. The enemy tried to convince me that no one would ever want to hear what I had to say. But au contraire. He is such a liar. The enemy tried to convince me that my marriage is over. But au contraire. He is such a liar. I may have believed that months ago, but not today. You see, the one thing my counselor prays for at the end of our sessions is that our marriage gets restored back to the place where God intended it to be. Not to where I want it to be. And, not even to the place where my husband wants it to be. But, to the place where God purposed it to be. Somehow along our journey, we let the distractions create a bridge between us. But God is a mender of bridges. Somewhere along the line, we let the holes and voids in our hearts be filled with emptiness. But God is a heart-fixer. Somewhere along the line, we let our 'perceptions' get the best of us. But God is a mind regulator, and He can renew a right spirit within us (Psalm 51: 10). There is no problem, no issue, no situation, that God cannot heal. Even if that means that you get up walking with a limp like Jacob (Genesis 32:25-31). God will honor your heart and your desire to stand in your truth. So, if you give it to Him, I guarantee restoration is in your future.

Chapter 17

Turning Around Your What-Nots...

Do you know that prayer is the answer to a lot of your problems? Think about this. How hard is it to 'find' the time to pray? You can have a time carved out that you are going to read your Word and pray, and low and behold, here comes a distraction. Your intentions are there. But there is always something that supersedes your efforts.

Especially when you are trying to make a deliberate effort to get closer to God. Now think about this. Why do you think the enemy fights you so hard for your prayer time? Because he knows the effects of prayer. The prayers of a righteous (i.e., upright, decent, virtuous, worthy) person are powerful and effective (James 5: 16). And one the most effectual "what-nots" I can give you is to pray. Pray without ceasing (1 Thessalonians 5:17). The enemy does not want you to pray. Because he knows that is one of our most effective weapons. One of the hardest things I did during my separation was pray for my marriage. Sounds crazy, huh? Well, let me explain. Because as we were separated, my husband and I did not speak. So, most of the time, I really did not even know what to pray for. I mean my whole world had just been turned upside down. The world I thought I would live in forever. The world I thought was pretty okay and do-able. So, I was a little stumped about what to even go to God for. I could pray for 'things' I thought needed healing.

But what if I prayed for the wrong thing' So. of course, I prayed. And, one day the Holy Spirit gave me instructions to have a funeral, or memorial service, for my marriage. Initially, I was thoroughly confused, but I listened intuitively. And the more I listened, the more instructions I received. So, one Saturday morning, I planned this funeral. I had picked out some music, an outfit, and the location (i.e., my living room). I did have two attendees: my two yorkies. At first, I felt obviously silly, but I hung in there and followed through. I had a picture of my husband and I in our early days that served as the program. Then, it became time to deliver the eulogy. I do not recall every single thing I said. But I do remember eulogizing the 'innocence' of the two people here in front of me. I was thankful for their history, their past. But I was eager for their future. And, before I realized it, I was praising God. Praising God for their union. Praising God for their love. Praising God for their promise. Praising God for their marriage. Then this acronym fell in my spirit---PICKLL. Yes, pronounced pickle. And this is what the Holy Spirit gave me. As I was praising God, He told me that the "P" is for passion. There are two facets to this 'passion.' The first passion is the most obvious. This was the sensual part of 'passion' that I sometimes restricted myself from engaging in. Passion that I was insecure about engaging in. Passion that I wanted with my husband. Passion that I now longed for with my husband. I wanted this man and I wanted him more than ever. I wanted my marriage to exude passion. Passion in our eyes. Passion in our touch. Passion in our words. Passion in our bodies. I wanted passion to be our unspoken language. And then there is the second facet to the word 'passion.' This passion is more spiritual because this is the passion that you are willing to fight for. This is the passion that you will endure struggling for. This is the passion that you are willing to suffer for. And I was passionate about suffering for what God says my marriage should be. The "I" is for intimacy. The Lord knew my struggle in this area, but He wanted me to be healed from all of my hurts. From all of my insecurities. From all of my vulnerabilities. From all of my deceptiveness in this area. Intimacy between a husband and wife is something that should be celebrated and remarkable. I wanted to be able to look across a crowded room and catch my husband's eye and he would FEEL the intimacy from my eyes. I wanted him to feel the depth of the love in my heart for him through our intimate moments. I belong to my beloved and his desire is for me (Song of Solomon 7:10). This was the level of intimacy I began praising God for. The "C" is for communication. I used to say, "What you see is what you get." But that statement had been so far from the truth. I had let you see the book, but you would never get the chance to scroll through my pages. Well, that day in my funeral, I began praising God for a different level of communication between my husband and me. During this season, God was giving me my voice. God was healing me through my pain. God was showing me that it was okay to be imperfect. God was showing me that it was okay to be flawed. His love covers my pain. His love covers my imperfections. His love covers my flaws. His love covered my silence when I did not know how to speak. His love showed me who I am in Him. And I wanted to scream it to the world how good God is! I know now I can trust. I know now I can love. I know now I can open up. I am not afraid anymore. I am not embarrassed anymore. I am not damaged anymore. I am not heartbroken anymore. I was ready and yearning to share. The "K" is for kissing. I praised God for more "sweet kissing" moments. Those unexpected moments. Those anticipated moments. Those moments filled with such spark, yet tenderness. I wanted a moment like in Song of Solomon 1:2, "Let him kiss me with the kisses of his mouth; for his love is more delightful than wine." I wanted 'sweet kisses' that would have me thinking about it all day. The first "L" is for laughter. Laughter is the best medicine for it draws people together in such a way that a unique bond is created. In our marriage, we had so many days and experiences filled with laughter. That was the glue that held us together when dealing with life. I was thankful for those times. But I began praising God for even better days. I began praising God that our latter days would be more bountiful than our former days (Haggai 2:9). I began praising God for more days filled with smiles. More days filled with laughter. More days filled with making memories. More days filled with embracing life's journey together, bringing the joy of laughter along the way. The last "L" is for love. I cannot speak for my husband, but I know I struggled in this area. Not because of anything he did or did not do. But it was me who held back. I tried to overcompensate by 'giving' in other ways. But all my husband wanted from me was my love. With God's help, I was healing through all my misperceptions about love. I was healing through all my perversions about love. I was healing through all my mistrusts about love. I knew I was not where I wanted to be. But I was thankful that I was not where I used to be. I began praising God for my Prayer of Jabez increase. God was enlarging my heart to be able to love. And to love uninhibitedly. Love unconditionally. Love uncondemningly. Love unblemished. Love non-judgmentally. God was showing me that I deserved to be loved. And that it was okay to show love. I began praising God for His unending love for me. I began praising God for showing me how a wife is to love her husband. I began praising God for showing me how to love myself; in my flaws and all. But it was God's abounding love for me that showed me how I needed to love in marriage. I think I said a closing prayer, and this now concluded the service. I realized that God had me to do this because I was having a hard time letting go of the past. And, if I was not willing to let go of the past, then I was not going to appreciate what was in front of me. You cannot move forward looking back. In my heart of hearts, I believe with everything in me that God was getting me ready for a new thing. And this was going to be something that I had never seen.

I am as far from perfect as the next person. But God has given me grace. Not because I have earned it, but because He loves me. And there is nothing we could ever do to deserve the love that God has for us. John 3:16 says, "For God so loved the world that He gave his one and only Son, that whoever believes in Him shall not perish but have eternal life." There is also John 15:13, "Greater love has no one than this: to lay down one's life for one's friends." God loves us. And no matter how hard you try; you will never be perfect. We all have flaws. We all make mistakes. We are all born in sin. You will make some choices in life that you will want to do-over. Not to burst your bubble, but you cannot. However, the silver lining is that you learn from your choices and do not make the same choice(s) again. That is the whole point of these little "what-nots." These are second chances (i.e., grace) that God gives us all of what not to do (i.e., "what-nots") in life, in love, in relationships, in marriage. You have heard me say it once, maybe twice, probably thrice, and I am going to keep saying it. The way for me to encourage you to be better is to tell you of those things of what not to do. Trust me, they will get you nowhere. The world can be stressful in itself. Marriage should not be. This is the one institution where you find solace. This is the one institution where you find respect. This is the one institution where you find support and encouragement. Marriage is what you make it. You have the power in your tongue to make your marriage what you call it, whether it is life or death (Proverbs 18:21). Even if your marriage is not where you want or like it to be, begin speaking your faith over it. Begin calling forth those things that are not as though they are (Romans 4: 17). And watch God move on your behalf.

Everything that I have gone through in my life, is my testimony. For every trial I faced, God gave me a testimony. For every test I faced, God gave me a way of escape. For every plan that the enemy used to keep me down, God reminded me that He created me to overcome. For all the 'bad' that I endured, God uses it for my good and His glory. For every immature act I displayed in my marriage, God grew me. For every demonstration of disrespect in my marriage, God purged me. For every sin I have committed, God has forgiven me. For every "what-not" act in my marriage, God has used to stretch me. Stretch me in my faith in Him. Stretch me in my trust in Him. Stretch me in my humility in Him. For all that I have done. For all the things I am guilty of. For all the things that I am ashamed of. God reminded me that His grace is sufficient. He is using my pain for His glory. He is using my shame for His glory. He is using my brokenness for His glory. He is using my heartbreak for His glory. And no matter how hard I may try, I am flawed. I will never be perfect. I will still make mistakes (Rest assured. I am steering away from those of my past). And, I will still have to own my truths. But the one thing I do know, is that God loves me. Crazy old me. And it is His perfect love that covers a perfectly flawed me.

Chapter 18

God Has A Reason For Everything...

I could sit up here and tell you all these reasons why I am doing what I am doing. Why I am writing what I am writing. Why I am sharing like I am sharing. But God has not given me the 'bigger picture' yet. But the truth is, God did not give me a revelation until finishing this book. It was not until I heard something on the tv that something began to stir in my spirit. Just keep Genesis 8:22 in the back of your mind for right now. And it reads, "As long as the earth endures, seedtime and harvest, will never cease." It will all tie in. The pieces will fit. But for now, as my spirit was getting stirred, God began speaking. And He told me, "That is why you do what you do. That is why you have to write the book. That is why you have to share your story." All the pieces WILL fit. Psalm 37:3 says, "Trust in the Lord and do good." There is a difference between trusting God to do something versus trusting God through something And this is where I was at. I was in a 'process' in my life. I was in a 'process' in my relationships. I was in a 'process' in my marriage. And I could say all day that I trusted God. But what was I doing? What was I doing in this process of trusting? The process is sometimes the hardest part. Trying to maintain your trust in God. It is during the process that everything looks still. It is during the process that you do not see any results. It is during the process that you do not see any activity. It is during the process that sometimes God may not speak. It is during the process that you can

133

feel hopeless. It is during the process that you want to give up because you cannot see an end in sight. It is also during the process that the enemy is CONSTANTLY in your ear provoking you to quit. Quit on yourself. Quit on your purpose. Quit on your relationship. Quit on your marriage. Quit on God. But then, God sends you a Word. A Word tailored made from heaven just for you. A tailor-made Word just for me. And that morning, I got my tailor-made Word. And that Word was, "You may not be able to fix your own situation. But you can sow a seed of goodness into someone else's relationship. Into someone else's marriage." That is why you are doing what you are doing. In the process of me waiting through my situation, I am going to do. This book is my seed. Just because my marriage is not where I want it to be does not mean that God still cannot use my testimony. Just because my marriage does not exemplify where I want it to be does not mean that God still is not good. I had to first TRUST God. Then I had to DO GOOD. And my doing good is an action. I am sowing. And I am going to keep on sowing.

Now, pull out that scripture I asked you to tuck away earlier. Genesis 8:22. Seedtime and harvest time will never cease. So, what the enemy tried to use as a set-back, God has turned around for a set-up in life. A set-up for His Glory to be magnified in my life. A set-up for His Purpose to be fulfilled through me. A setup for His Demonstration of Grace that will be evident in my life. Ultimately, I am being set-up for a different kind of harvest. The harvest God intended for me. And not the harvest I tried to manipulate. With this harvest, I know Who I am building my house on. With this harvest, I know Who is responsible. With this harvest, I know Who will get the glory. The first time, my house was not built on the Word of God. It may have even been built on the word of Tena. And as you can see that foundation was unstable. Whatever I built on top of that got shook up. Whatever I built on top of that cracked and ultimately collapsed. Destroying everything that was on that foundation. Psalm 127:1 says, "Unless the Lord builds the house, those who build it labor in vain." But. And there's ALWAYS a but with God. Not because I deserve it. But because HE IS SO GOOD, GRACIOUS, and MERCIFUL. And because I am here today, that indicates to me that my purpose is not yet fulfilled.

Because I am here today, that indicates to me that God is not done with me yet. Because I am here today, that indicates to me that God IS a God of second chances. And, whatever God's Will is for my life, I will trust Him.

Staying Joyfully Married ... My little book of "What-Nots," is a book of truths. This is a book about healing. This is a book about restoration. This is a book about redemption. This is a 'big reveal' book. The 'big reveal' of the new 'GodGraced' Me. The 'big reveal' of God's Hand demonstrated over my life. The 'big reveal' of God's Kindness. The 'big reveal' that God can still use me.

God has been many different things to me in my life. But, if you have never experienced Him as a Healer, you can only go by here-say. If you have never known God as a Way-Maker, you can only go by here-say. And do not get me wrong. That is the purpose of sharing our testimonies. For The Word tells us in Revelation 12:11 that they (we) overcome by the word of each other's testimony. But when you have to find out for yourself that God is a Healer. When you have to find out for yourself that God is a WayMaker. Your testimony becomes different. Your testimony becomes personal. And it does not matter what no one says. When you know that you know what you know, no one can tell you any different. You are convinced. You are determined. You are matter-of-fact.

During this season of my life, I have become convinced. Convinced that God is REAL. Convinced that God is NEVER CHANGING. Convinced that God is MERCIFUL. Convinced that God is a HEART-FIXER. Convinced that God is a MIND-REGULATOR. Convinced that God is a RENEWER. Convinced that God is OMNISCIENT. This season has become my testimony. My testimony that God can use even me in my mistakes. My testimony that God can use even me in my brokenness. My testimony that God can use even me in my insecurities. My testimony that God can use even me in my vulnerabilities. My testimony that God can use even me in my self-sabotaging choices. My daily confession is, "Thank you God that I am continuing to become. I do not know what my future holds, but I know Who holds my future. And I anxiously await further 'big reveals' in my life."

Conclusion

I Am Picture Perfect...

When God first gave me this title, I was com pletely baffled. And to be honest, even as I wrote, I still was not in complete agreement about it.

However, it was not until I was talking to some one and I was expressing my insecurity about not only the title, but its contents, that I got what I needed. And that is when the revelation was explained to me. Staying Joyfully Married... My Little Book of "What-Nots," is a self-reflection book about 'what not' to do in marriage, to help you stay more joyful in marriage. I may not be able to tell a person what to do to stay joyfully married. But I can share those things that will not contribute to you staying joyfully married. Those things that I learned along my journey that did not aid in mymarriage growing and becoming stronger in God and in love. A book of mistakes. A book of lessons. A book that will hopefully prevent he next person from making the same mistakes that I made. A book that will hopefully make you think twice before you say or act. A book that will hopefully encourage you to look at your mar riage in a different light. A book that will hope fully help you embrace the love of your life the way God intended for love to be shown between two people. If I have said it once, I am going to keep on saying it. I do not want you to be like me. And please, do not try to be better than me. You cannot fill my shoes and I know I cannot fill yours. My prayer for you is that you allow God to make you into the bestest version of you that He intended for you to be.

I would like to leave you with a little word of encouragement. You are valuable. You are worthy. You are God's Masterpiece (Ephesians 2:10). You are not your mistakes. Ask for repent ance. Learn from them. And keep walking one faith-filled step at a time. And just remember, the same grace you have been given, give it. Stay humble and continue to become all that God says you are. God has given you grace to grow This blessed me and my prayer is that it blesses you as well. As I was listening to ministry tv one morning, I was intrigued by a tes- timony one of the minister's was sharing. He talked about how there was a Picasso painting called 'The Dream' that sold for $SO million dollars. The buyer, after a few years, decided to flip the deal and sell the painting. The deal was in place. The bid was accepted. And everyone was celebrating because of this exchange which was about to take place for $139 million dollars. Well, somehow in the midst of celebrating and party- ing, the buyer accidentally bumped into the painting and tore it. He was devastated, not only because he was not going to make a profit off his investment. But, in his mind, he would never now make a profit because he saw this painting as permanently damaged. He reluctantly sought out what is called an 'art surgeon' for assistance. To his surprise, this surgeon asked for at least a year to work on it and try to repair it. To try and restore it to its original beauty. Well, to the buyer's surprise, this art surgeon ended up repairing 'The Dream.' And did so to a state where it was described by experts, as being technically a restoration of beauty. Ultimately, this looked to be a win-win situation. Not only was 'The Dream' restored, but the buyer ended up selling it for more than the original offer of $139 mil- lion dollars. He sold 'The Dream' for $150 million dollars.

As I was sitting there listening to this mes- sage, my spirit was getting stirred, and tears began rolling down my cheeks. God uses such simplistic revelations to speak. And what He told was humbling. And this is just how I was told the revelation. You see, to the naked eye, this paint- ing, 'The Dream,' looked flawless. This painting had such impeccable beauty. It did not look like the trauma it had just been through. However, if you turned the painting around, that is when you saw its scars. That is when you saw that it was not perfect. That is when you became aston- ished by knowing the process this painting had been through. The despair this painting had been through. The complexities this painting had been through. The brokenness this painting had been through. The heartbreak this painting had been through. This painting, 'The Dream,' was me and the process I had been, and was, still going through. No, it was not evident what I was going through. No, it was not even evident what I had been through. But, if you turned me around, you would see my scars. If you turned me around, you would see my imperfections. If you turned me around, you would see my mis- takes. If you turned me around, you would see just how flawed I really was. But. And there is always a but. Just like with this painting 'The Dream,' this art surgeon had not only restored this painting to a place where it was purposed to be. Thereby increasing the value of this painting beyond its original value. But it was somehow more valuable now than when it was first bought. Your pearl for the day: It does not matter what you go through in life. It does not matter how defeated you may even feel. When God restores you, He not only restores you to the place where He intended you to be. But you also come out more valuable. The Word says that by His stripes, we are healed. If you turn Christ over, you will see the stripes He took for you. If you turn Christ over, you will see stripes of healing. If you turn Chris over, you will see stripes of restoration. If you turn Christ over, you will see stripes of new beginnings. If you turn Christ over, you will see stripes of second chances. If you turn Christ over, you will see His stripes of love that He took for you and for me. The same way that Picasso's painting, 'The Dream,' got redeemed to a value better than when it was created, is the same way God wants to redeem you. God did not create us to live in failures. God did not create us to just be average. God did not create us not to live in His Glory. The same way the art surgeon restored 'The Dream' is the same way that God wants to restore you. It is the same way God wants to restore me. For every set back in your life, Christ has already taken a stripe. For every delay in your life, Christ has already taken a stripe. For every wrong turn in your life, Christ has already taken a stripe. For every mistake in your life, Christ has already taken a stripe. For every ounce of trouble in your life, Christ has already taken a stripe. For every affliction in your life, Christ has already taken a stripe. Can we be honest? If we did not have trouble in our lives, we would not know how to trust God. We would not have a reason to. Did you know that affliction leads to increase? Read about David in Psalms 119:71 or read about James in chapter 1:2-3. Or how about we ice things off by reading John 16:33. Affliction builds your faith in God. But, getting back to the Picasso painting, if this meticulous, strategic, and patient art surgeon could put back together a painting worth over $150 million dollars, a painting that he did not even create, what do you think our Master Surgeon, The One who created us, can do? The One who put His DNA on the inside of each and every one of us. The One we call Abba, Our Heavenly Father, wants to heal, repair, and restore every aspect of our lives. It is okay to turn around. You do not have to hide your scars. God will trade you His beauty for your ashes (Isaiah 61 :3).